The Brief Life & Mysterious Death of Boris III, King of Bulgaria

Sasha Wilson & Joseph Cullen

Further devised by
Out Of The Forest Theatre

methuen | drama
LONDON • NEW YORK • OXFORD • NEW DELHI • SYDNEY

METHUEN DRAMA
Bloomsbury Publishing Plc
50 Bedford Square, London, WC1B 3DP, UK
1385 Broadway, New York, NY 10018, USA
29 Earlsfort Terrace, Dublin 2, Ireland

BLOOMSBURY, METHUEN DRAMA and the Methuen
Drama logo are trademarks of Bloomsbury Publishing Plc

First published in Great Britain 2024

A catalogue record for this book is available from the British Library.

A catalog record for this book is available from the Library of Congress.

ISBN: PB: 978-1-3505-1272-6
ePDF: 978-1-3505-1273-3
eBook: 978-1-3505-1274-0

Series: Modern Plays

Typeset by Mark Heslington Ltd, Scarborough, North Yorkshire

To find out more about our authors and books visit
www.bloomsbury.com and sign up for our newsletters.

The Brief Life & Mysterious Death of Boris III, King of Bulgaria

Written by Sasha Wilson & Joseph Cullen

Further Devised by The Company
Dramaturgy by Hannah Hauer-King
Produced by Out Of The Forest Theatre

LIST OF CREDITS

Writers – Sasha Wilson & Joseph Cullen

Director & Dramaturg – Hannah Hauer-King

Ensemble – Lawrence Boothman, Joseph Cullen, Clare Fraenkel, David Leopold & Sasha Wilson

Producer – Claire Gilbert

Assistant Producer – Lorra Videv

Stage Manager – Zoë Mackinnon

Lighting Designer – Will Alder

Set Designer – Sorcha Corcoran

Costume Designer – Helen Stewart

Music Consultant – Dessi Stefanova

In association with Something for the Weekend.

The above cast performed the show at Pleasance Theatre, Edinburgh in 2023 and at Arcola Theatre, London in 2023 as well as 59E59 Theaters, New York in 2024. They won the Best Performance Ensemble Award at the Off West End Awards 2024.

Previous team:

Ensemble – Joseph Prowen & Kara Taylor Alberts

Stage Manager – Maddie Whiffin

Cover image credit – Photographs by Héctor Manchego, design by Desk Tidy.

ON THE HISTORY OF THE SHOW

In 2017 co-writers Sasha Wilson and Joseph Cullen went to Cleveland, Ohio to visit Sasha's grandparents ('O'papa' and 'O'mama' as she called them), who had fled Bulgaria and what was then Yugoslavia respectively during the war. Both made wild, peripatetic journeys through a ravaged Europe until they met each other in an internment camp in Trieste, Italy. They married and had such a raucous wedding party that they damaged the walls of the barracks in which they were living. In the rubble, they found bits of silver twisted up in tissue paper. It was enough to buy each other wedding rings and passage to the States. But they never forgot the Balkans. On their bookshelf was a copy of Stephane Groueff's *Crown of Thorns*, a biography of Boris III of Bulgaria. The idea for *The Brief Life & Mysterious Death of Boris III, King of Bulgaria* was born, and selected for VAULT Festival 2020 in London, where it won an Origins Award for outstanding new work. Six shows were performed in March 2020, just before the first Covid-19 lockdown. They were supported in January 2023 by ACE to further R&D the show. The company performed twenty-six shows at the Pleasance, Edinburgh Festival Fringe 2023 (where it came 2nd Runner Up in the BBC and Popcorn Group's New Writing Award), and one performance at the Bulgarian Embassy in London, with a subsequent transfer to the Arcola, London for another twenty-seven performances. 2024 saw the show transfer to 59E59 Theaters in New York.

WRITERS' NOTE

When you learn history at school, it's easy to be misled into believing that it is a simple series of concrete facts passed on; lists of kings and queens and military battles that march imperviously through the pages of a textbook. But in reality historical accounts don't follow clear linear narratives. There are always facts that are ignored and perspectives that are imposed. What you choose to include or omit dramatically shapes the overall picture.

Take the Second World War, for example. It is a subject matter for which the UK has an apparently bottomless appetite. Co-writer Joseph grew up in Somerset on a healthy diet of *Dad's Army* and *Blackadder* (which are still often performed on rural am-dram stages – to great reviews!). But mention Bulgaria and many people will think first of *The Wombles* or Viktor Krum from *Harry Potter*. Fair to say plenty may struggle to point at Bulgaria on a map, let alone be aware that nearly 50,000 Jewish Bulgarians were saved from deportation and death. Co-writer Sasha is American-Bulgarian, and had never heard of King Boris III until her O'papa gave her a copy of *Crown of Thorns*. We were staggered that despite our many nerdy friends and our shared history-buffness, nobody we knew seemed to have heard this story. So we dived right into a mountain of research.

What became immediately apparent is that this was not just another straightforward tale of goodies beating baddies. This was a more thorny and instructive tale for our times. What struck us was the everyday heroism of what Michael Bar-Zohar (author of *Beyond Hitler's Grasp*) calls the 'extraordinary ordinary people'. This isn't a hagiography of a monarch, but rather a tale that details how Bulgarian citizens, everyday people like you or me, looked around their society and decided to make a stand for what they believed in.

Though it is ultimately a hopeful story, there is a profound central tragedy. There is scholarship that suggests Bulgaria wished to remain neutral in the conflict after the devastation of the First World War. Ultimately, the country was too militarily weak not to 'pick a side'. In an attempt to avoid invasion and regain territory, Bulgaria sided with Nazi Germany. This is not glamorous and this is not noble. But there it is. Bulgaria wanted to reclaim the territories of

Thrace and Macedonia and they were able to achieve that through siding with the Axis Powers. However, those territories were not entirely under their control until after the war. As a result, 11,343 Thracian and Macedonian men, women and children were rounded up and sent to Treblinka. Tragically, only twelve survived. This fact remains a stain on Bulgaria and on Boris III to this day. We do not in any way shy away from this in our production.

We can hold the complexity about both of these truths. We can marvel at the bravery of people like Liliana Panitsa, the secretary to the Head of The Commissariat for Jewish Questions, who smuggled information to Jewish families to evade arrest. Or the interventions of Metropolitan Stefan who harboured Jewish families in monasteries across Bulgaria. Jacky Comforty's documentary *The Optimists* interviews many Bulgarians who did as much as they could to intervene (wonderful viewing by the way). Following these events the royal family were exiled, and Bulgaria was invaded by the Soviets – so much information was covered up, and it is only in the last couple of decades that resources have become available.

Our interest as a theatre company is to meta-theatrically 'show our work' and let people in on the nuance and conflicting information within the process of storytelling. Ultimately, we are making a play so we have made certain artistic decisions. For example, that Boris put the 20,000 Jewish Bulgarians into labour camps *so* that they wouldn't be sent abroad to their deaths. We can't know for sure of his intentions, but we open our research up to you, and in so doing we interrogate how the stories we tell shape who we are.

DIRECTOR'S NOTE

How do you talk about the 1940s and the Second World War without saying what's been said before? How do you not just echo the 'Britain and the Allies vanquishing Germany' narrative, or fall into uncomfortable generalisations or even clichés about such a painful and obsessed-upon period of history? How do you talk about the Jewish experience within that in a way that is theatrically satisfying and entertaining, whilst honouring the trauma of that time?

If you'd asked me this five years ago, I wouldn't have answered 'through the lens of King Boris III of Bulgaria'. In fact I hadn't even heard of him, despite his saving nearly 50,000 Jewish Bulgarians, and as a granddaughter of a Polish Jew, I expect saving many of my not too far removed ancestors.

And yet he presents the perfect protagonist to talk about this part of history, but from the unheard perspective of Bulgaria. A fundamentally flawed, avoidant, boisterous and also brave king who wasn't even Bulgarian 'by blood', whatever that means. As a company we have relished portraying his bravery and silliness, and his contradictions. But even more, we enjoyed celebrating the courageous voices that surrounded him, who are even less remembered.

One important stylistic decision has been the portrayal of Nazi war criminals, or indeed Hitler himself. I'm always a little wary about portrayals of Nazis on stage, and I'm often left contemplating what's being achieved after seeing yet another bad Hitler moustache or sewn-together swastika. I feel proud of the decision the company made to not embody Hitler, and to avoid swastika iconography. The horror of the impact of these figures is no less, and we can rely on performance and audience imagination, not '*heils*' and icons, to speak to this horror.

But though the piece certainly does not shy away from the trauma at the time, you will also find that there is plenty of humour and 'poking fun' at the absurdity and bigotry of certain characters. Of course, there's a careful balance between satire and making light of the horrific; holding the moments of despair, whilst also finding that humour. And that humour and playfulness, alongside an unwavering seriousness about loss of human life and suffering, feels like a crucial part of the gesture of this piece.

And hope. Though violence and hate are featured in this story, the story that prevails and that we wanted to tell is of the often unsung heroes who did their bit and spoke out. Hearing and bringing life to their stories on stage gives me hope for the people now who speak up today.

OUT OF THE FOREST THEATRE

Out Of The Forest Theatre is a multi-award-winning ensemble-based company. We take misremembered or forgotten stories from history, set them to live folk music, and tell them through a lens to better understand today. Irreverently presented, knee-slapping, historical theatre with a modern revisionist twist. Previous productions include *Bury The Hatchet* – winner of Best Ensemble at Off West End Awards; *Call Me Fury* – winner of Alchymy Award; *Louisa & Jo (& Me)*.

The company was founded in 2018 by Sasha Wilson, Joseph Cullen and Claire Gilbert. In 2023 they appointed David Leopold as their first Associate Artist.

COMPANY BIOGRAPHIES

Sasha Wilson (co-Writer, Actor – Giovanna, Dannecker, Liliana Panitsa)

Sasha is a Bulgarian-American LAMDA-trained actor. **Recent credits include**: *A Christmas Carol* (Taunton Brewhouse); *Noises Off* (Beck Center for the Arts); *The Tempest* (Shakespeare in the Squares); *The Mechanicals Present: Julius Caesar or Macbeth* (UK tour). Winner of 2018 Broadway World Award for Best Actress in a Play for *Romeo and Juliet* (Southwest Shakespeare Company). **For the company**: *Bury The Hatchet* (VAULT Festival, Hope Theatre, US tour); *Call Me Fury* (VAULT Festival, Hope Theatre) and *Louisa & Jo (& Me)* (Golden Goose). Sasha is also the Artistic Director of Out Of The Forest Theatre.

Joseph Cullen (co-Writer, Actor – Boris III)

Joseph is an actor, writer and producer from south Somerset; his love for theatre began at a young age with amateur dramatics and community shows. **Recent credits include**: *The Darklings* (VAULT Festival); *Alice's Adventures Underground*, *The Game's Afoot* (Les Enfants Terribles); *Twelfth Night*, *The Three Musketeers* (Southwest Shakespeare Company). Joseph is also the Executive Producer of Out Of The Forest Theatre.

Hannah Hauer-King (Dramaturg, Director)

Hannah is a director and dramaturg, with a focus on new writing, LGBTQIA+ work and musicals. She is Artistic Director of theatre company Damsel Productions, and currently works as Resident Director at the National Theatre Studio. **Recent directing credits include**: *The Swell* (Orange Tree Theatre) – Olivier Award nominated; *The Ministry of Lesbian Affairs*, *Fabric*, *Fury* (Soho Theatre); *The Funeral Director* (Southwark Playhouse/English Touring Theatre UK tour); *The Amber Trap* (Theatre503); *Dry Land* (Jermyn Street Theatre). **For the company**: *Call Me Fury* (Hope Theatre);

Louisa & Jo (& Me) (Golden Goose). **Associate/Assistant credits include**: *The Wife of Willesden* (Kiln Theatre, BAM & ART); *Romeo and Juliet* (Shakespeare's Globe); *Daytona* (Park Theatre, Theatre Royal Haymarket).

Lawrence Boothman (Actor – Filov)

Lawrence studied at the Music School of Douglas Academy in Milngavie and holds an MA in Acting from the Royal Conservatoire of Scotland. **Recent credits include**; *Jack* (Òran Mór, Traverse Theatre, Macrobert Arts Centre); *Ode to Joy (How Gordon Got to Go to the Nasty Pig Party)* (Sydney Festival); *The Devil Drinks Cava* (Òran Mór); *Julius Caesar* (Scottish tour); *The Odyssey* (The Scoop); *Incident at Vichy* (Finborough Theatre).

Clare Fraenkel (Actor – Gabrovski, Anka Lazarov)

Clare studied English at Bristol University, then trained at Drama Studio London. An actor, puppeteer and writer, her autobiographical show is entitled *I Was a German*. **Recent credits include**: *I Was a German* (VAULT Festival) – nominated for Off West End Award; *Against Democracy* (Arcola Theatre); *Girl with the Iron Claws* (Soho Theatre & tour); *Wolves of Willoughby Chase* (UK tour); *Rough Music* (King's Head); *The Borrowers* (Haymarket – Basingstoke); *The Rivals* (UK tour); multiple productions and tours for Polka Theatre and Oxford Shakespeare Company. **Screen credits include**: *This Is Going to Hurt* (BBC); *Magic Mike's Last Dance* (Warner Bros).

David Leopold (Associate Artist, Actor – Belev, Metropolitan Stefan)

David trained at LAMDA. Upon graduating, he was selected for the Graduate Actors Scheme at Leeds Playhouse. **Recent credits include**: *Late Company* (Trafalgar Studios, Finborough Theatre); *Burnt Part Boys* (Park Theatre); *Little Sure Shot* (The Egg – Theatre Royal Bath); *Uncle Vanya, The*

Crucible (Leeds Playhouse). **For the company**: *Bury The Hatchet* (Hope Theatre); *Louisa & Jo (& Me)* (Golden Goose). **Screen credits include**: *The Angel* (Netflix). Also a singer/songwriter, David released his debut EP *Lost on Abbotswood* in 2023.

WITH THANKS

With thanks to the team at 59E59 Theaters, Arcola Theatre, Bulgarian Embassy (London), Arts Council England, US Embassy (London), HRH Prince Kyril of Bulgaria & Katharine Butler, HRH Crown Prince Boris of Bulgaria, Anthony Alderson & Nic Connaughton, Pleasance Theatre, Chloe Nelkin PR, VAULT Festival, Suzanna Rosenthal, Charlotte Lund, Jennifer Amey, Judith Dimant, Nancy Stewart, Stage One, Riverside Studios, James Bulgin and the Imperial War Museum, Tristan Tull and Regents Park University, Hugh Edwards and Reigate Grammar School, Steve Dykes and Rose Bruford College of Theatre and Performance, Paul Anderson and Sparks Theatrical Hires, Althea Theatre, Callan McCarthy and Methuen Drama, Becky Bainbridge, Holly Ellis, Françoise Davis, Axel Veerkamp, Aydan Wilder, Will McLeod, Debra Hauer and Westminster Synagogue, Eliana Ostro, Geargin Wilson, Christina Gelev, Tom Williams, Rosie Bauer, Brian Williams, Carolyn Williams, Helen Gilbert, Paul Gilbert, Louise & Matt Phillips, Abi Matthews, Callum Patrick Hughes, David Shopland, Georgia Harris, John Wakefield, Zdravka Momcheva, Wassil Rascheeff and to O'papa who inspired the story – лека му пръст.

The Brief Life & Mysterious Death of Boris III, King of Bulgaria

Cast List

Actor 1/Boris III
Actor 2/Giovanna, Dannecker, Liliana Panitsa, German Emissary, Soviet Apparatchik
Actor 3/Filov, French Emissary, Ferdinand I
Actor 4/Belev, Metropolitan Stefan, Advisor 3, Austr(al)ian Emissary
Actor 5/Gabrovski, Anka Lazarov, Bulgarian Emissary, Convert, Factory Worker[1]

Dramatis Personae

Boris III, *King of Bulgaria*
Giovanna, *Queen of Bulgaria*
Filov, *Prime Minister*
Gabrovski, *Minister of the Interior*
Belev, *Head of the Commissariat of Jewish Questions*
Liliana Panitsa, *Belev's secretary*
Anka Lazarov, *a musician turned activist*
Metropolitan Stefan, *Head of the Bulgarian Orthodox Church*
Dannecker, *Captain of Hitler's SS*

Hitler *to be 'played' by a hat stand adorned with coat and hat.*[2]

Radio Broadcasts *to be read live in a shared 'cod-1940s British newscaster' voice by different cast members in turn.*

List of Songs

'Mila Rodino' (Bulgarian national anthem)
'This Land Is Your Land'
'Bella Ciao'
'Bei Mir Bist Du Schoen'
'Minor Swing'

---

[1] The original company of actors played mandolin (Actor 2), guitar (Actor 3), violin (Actor 4) and flute (Actor 5). We found the character of Filov particularly suits being played by a violinist, but feel free to experiment and build your own band. Boris does not sing or play, to retain the authority of this character. 'The King's Players', as they are referred to, will provide all musical accompaniment.
[2] Please do not use any swastikas, Totenkopfs or Nazi insignias in any of the costume pieces. They aren't necessary and we want to avoid festishising these symbols of fear.

'Shalom Aleichem'
'Avinu Malkeinu'
'Have A Little Talk With Jesus'
'Which Side Are You On?'
'Kaval Sviri'

A Note on the Ensemble

*The **Ensemble** conjures the world of the play and guides the audience through it. They are there to tease, to clarify, to inform. They work as a unit and fun can be had through passing instruments and bits of costume to each other, which offers a 'rough-and-readiness' to the piece. Like a soccer team or a corps de ballet, they physically move together and support each other. Ultimately and most importantly, they love this story and are passing it on to the audience with joy, sincerity and plenty of humour. They take the work seriously but not themselves. They are comic and self-aware but they never undermine the gravity and relevance of the story they are trying to tell. There's a spring in the step and a glint in the eye but the line between comedy and drama is trodden finely and that line is always being questioned and interrogated.*

A Note on the Musical Language

You'll notice the musical choices ricochet from traditional Bulgarian songs to Jewish music sung in prayer, as well as other folk numbers of the time. The realising of this music has truly been a collaborative effort, including the help of Dessi Stefanova (London Bulgarian Choir), David Leopold (Associate Artist), and Westminster Synagogue, from whom director Hannah Hauer-King learned the two Jewish tunes. The music is the soundtrack to the play. It changes the emotional state of the scene or allows the audience to breathe and metabolise information. Music intervenes when language does not suffice. To clarify, this is a play with music (not a musical), and (with the exception of 'Have A Little Talk With Jesus' which was accompanied on the guitar and sung by Actor 4 as Metropolitan Stefan) the characters within the world of the play don't spontaneously break into song, but the ensemble as the storytellers do. It is important to note as well that the chords or motifs for the songs can be incorporated at any point to serve as underscoring for scenes and we often punctuate scenic beats with musical stings. Consider the words of the scenes like a score and the music will slot right in.

Prologue

We start in blackness. The following **Radio Broadcast** *is played:*

Radio #1 (**Actor 1**) Good afternoon. This is a Radio Broadcast from 'Europe at War'. Welcome to [insert name of theatre] and Out Of The Forest Theatre's production[3] of *The Brief Life & Mysterious Death of Boris III, King of Bulgaria*. The year is 1943 – therefore, we ask that you turn off your mobile telephones. OFF. Or at the very least put them on airplane mode, the chaps at the RAF will thank you. Keep calm, carry on and do try to have a nice time. Don't worry, it'll all be over by Christmas.[4] Now to Bulgaria.

A heroic funereal opening of 'Mila Rodino' sung a capella in harmony shakes the foundations of the space.

Mila Rodino,	Dear Motherland,
ti si zemen raj,	you are heaven on earth,
tvojta hubost,	your beauty,
tvojta prelest,	your loveliness,
ah, te njamat kraj.	ah, they have no end.

The instruments join in.

Gorda Stara planina,	Proud Balkan Mountains,
do nej Dunava sinej,	next to it the Danube sparkles,
slynce Trakija ogrjava,	the sun lights up Thrace,
nad Pirina plamenej.	and blazes over Pirin.

Boris *enters – at the same level as the audience, he is a 'man of the people'.*

Mila Rodino,	Dear Motherland,
ti si zemen raj,	you are heaven on earth,
tvojta hubost,	your beauty,

---

[3] When this Radio Broadcast is recorded, it can be reworded to include the name of the company/group performing the play.

[4] This is a nod to an iconic phrase often used during the First World War to describe how long they predicted the conflict would last. Instead of 'Christmas' you may wish to say 'in ninety minutes' or 'in about an hour and a half' – something a little lighthearted to put the audience at ease.

> *tvojta prelest,*　　　　　　　your loveliness,
> *ah, te njamat kraj.*　　　　　ah, they have no end.

Boris *addresses his adoring public – the* **Ensemble** *vamp an underscore of 'Mila Rodino'.*

Boris　Welcome to the fairy-tale Kingdom of Bulgaria. This is the national anthem.

Actor 2　The current national anthem.

Actor 5　They had a different national anthem during World War II when this play is set.

Actor 4　This one was adopted in 1947.

Actor 3　We do know that by the way.

Boris　But I preferred this one, so I made an artistic choice.

All (*crescendo sing*)　　*RODINO*

Music returns to underscore vamp.

Boris　And I am Boris III, the penultimate king of Bulgaria. And the only reigning monarch in Nazi-occupied or Nazi-allied Europe /

Actor 5　Apart from Christian X of Denmark /

Boris　– enough about him! / Who refused to deliver the Jewish population to Hitler . . . (*Beat.*) I saved nearly 50,000 lives, and most of you have never bloody heard of me.

Actor 3　You think *you* won the war.

Actor 5　You beat the baddies.

Actor 4　You fought them on the beaches.

Actor 2　You fought them in the trenches –

Boris　And you won. And you made Dad's Army and the last scene of Blackadder[5] so you wouldn't forget you won. But this is Bulgaria's victory. And these are The King's Players.

---

[5] The last episode of *Blackadder* is actually about the First World War, not the Second. We do know that by the way, but it speaks to a British obsession with their own exceptionalism and relationship to Germany that is often encapsulated in the phrase, 'Two world wars and one world cup doo dah doo dah!'

All (*overlapping and individualised to each chorus voice*)   Hallo!

Boris (*delighted by the magic of theatre, won't this be fun!*)
They'll be playing all the other people in my life.

Actor 2   Playing important historical figures in their own right.

Boris   But with me – on the throne – as the protagonist.

Actor 2   We tried centring female narratives but, turns out, doesn't sell.

Music crashes to a stop. **Actor 4** *brings focus back to audience.*

Actor 4 (*big smile – salesman, back to the important stuff*)   Our play begins in 1943.

Actor 5   World War II is already under way.

Actor 3   So we will have to introduce you to some truly awful people.

Actor 2   But rest assured, this story isn't about them.

Actor 4   It's about the good people who stood up to them.

Boris   And everything you are about to see is true.

Ensemble *looks at* **Boris** *with a head snap; he smiles knowingly as we've taken a fair amount of artistic licence.*[6]

Ensemble *sing enthusiastically, with instruments.*

Rodino!	Motherland!
Mila Rodino,	Dear Motherland,
ti si zemen raj,	you are heaven on earth,
tvojta hubost,	your beauty,
tvojta prelest,	your loveliness,
ah, te njamat kraj.	ah, they are boundless.

---

[6] Where we *have* played a little fast and loose with compressing timelines and eliding characters, we have endeavoured to retain a certain spiritual truth (there's a lot we had to miss out!). We do let the audience *know* when we have done this (e.g. the anachronism of that version of the national anthem).

Covered by the music, **Boris** *and* **Ensemble** *move into positions for the opening boardroom scene.*

Scene One

Laying The Political Map

Boris   Right.

All *click heels in unison.*

Boris (*to the room*)   Where are we?

Advisor 3   A nondescript parliamentary briefing room in Bulgaria's capital city Sofia,[7] sir.

Boris   Well, then, welcome various white gentlemen with decision-making power you've almost certainly not earned. Prime Minister –

Filov   Yes, sire.

Boris   Home Secretary.

Gabrovski   So they tell me.

Boris   Lovely to see you both. What's the occasion?

Filov   War, your majesty.

Gabrovski   Gotta pick a team.

Boris   Can't we just bat for neutrality?

Filov   That's not really an option.

Gabrovski   Germany have a real powerhouse squad, sir.

Boris   And we don't?

Filov   No.

Gabrovski   They've already taken over most of Europe.

Boris   Well, who's left standing?

---

[7] The stress falls on the first syllable: Sofia.

Filov   Switzerland, Sweden. And the Irish.

Boris   Oh, the Irish? Well done them.

Filov   The Allies do want us on side, sir. But consider, the German forces have so far invaded Poland, Denmark, Norway, Belgium, the Netherlands, France. And oh here – Luxembourg.

Advisor 3   Luxem-where?

Boris (*noticing* **Advisor 3** *for the first time*)   Who are you?

Advisor 3   I'm Advisor Number 3.

Boris   Ah – well done. Now then what do we, Bulgaria, want?

Gabrovski   Get our country back!

Filov   The territory your father conceded.

Gabrovski   In the first war.

Filov   Southern Dobrudja, Macedonia and Thrace.

Advisor 3   The land your father lost.

Gabrovski   Your dad.

Advisor 3   Your dad.

Filov   Your dad.

Advisor 3   Make Bulgaria Great Again!

Filov   Bulgaria on three seas![8]

Gabrovski   Blue passports![9]

Boris   Yes thank you! You're all just shouting slogans at me now. Look, I appreciate we want our lands back, but we must do it without fighting. I want no loss of Bulgarian life in this war.

---

[8] България на три морета: The Black Sea, the Aegean Sea and the Adriatic Sea. An actual twentieth-century nationalist slogan for those wanting to return Bulgaria to its former glory, i.e. its historic borders during the Second Bulgarian Empire under the rule of Tsar Ivan (1218–41). *Street Without a Name* by Kapka Kassabova.

[9] Small lines like this can be updated to reflect the boneheaded Brexit-supporting equivalent of the time and place this is being performed.

Filov   You would like to side with *other* countries to help us get *our* land back?

Boris   Yes please.

Filov   Without our involvement?

Boris (*fingers crossed*)   It's worth a try. So for that we will need an ally, but who?

Advisor 3   Italy.

Filov   The Italians don't like us.

Advisor 3   Fuck Italy!

Boris   My wife is Italian.

Gabrovski   Yugoslavia?

Filov   They *really* don't like us.

Gabrovski   Fuck Yugoslavia.

Boris   Turkey?

Filov   We will *never* side with Turkey!

All *spit in unison.*

Beat.

Boris   What about the British?

Gabrovski   They're all the way on the other side of the English Channel.

Boris   The French?

Advisor 3   Right side of the Channel, sir, but they are pretty *occupied* with the Germans at the minute.

Filov (*wants **Boris** to side with the Germans but doesn't wish to tip his hand*)   The Germans *would* help us, but they might want us to co-invade the Soviet Union.

Advisor 3   But the Russians saved us from the vile and oppressive Turks.

All *spit.*

Boris   So to synthesise – (*Takes a deep breath.*) The French are occupied, the Italians don't like us. The Russians *would* help us take back Southern Dobrudja from Romania but they *won't* help us take back Macedonia from Yugoslavia because they don't want to tear Yugoslavia apart. The Germans will get us *all* the land we want, but they'll make us fight alongside them, and we won't fight the Russians, who the Germans want to fight. Joining the Germans could risk a British offensive, which we definitely don't want, but if we don't side with Germany they definitely will invade us like they have everywhere else . . .

(*Exhales. Gives withering look to audience – as if to say 'confusing right?'*) Gosh. So it's a close call, chaps, but I do think on this occasion it *has* to be the Nazis. I don't like it, but there is very little I do like at the moment, the world the way it is.

Advisor 3   You like hiking, sir. And yoga.

Boris   And the very end of meetings when everybody leaves.

All *click heels in unison,* **Advisor 3** *and* **Gabrovski** *exit.*

Scene Two

Boris Has Doubts

Filov *remains onstage with* **Boris**.

Filov   Your majesty, may I commend you on your excellent choice of ally. Cunning statecraft. If you don't mind my saying so, your father would have been proud.

Boris   Filov, between you and me and the Bulgarian gatepost, if I must be king – I really was rather hoping I could leave most of the politicking up to your lot.

Filov   The burden can be removed, sir. Should you choose it. Like your father – he chose to relinquish his monarchical authority.

Boris   Oh he always did enjoy giving things back. You know we once sent him a basket of mangoes for his birthday, obviously not to his taste, they were returned with a little note: 'these mangoes are completely pointless!'[10]

Filov (*deadpan*)   Ovoid objects often are.

Boris   I should just throw in the towel like Papa. He wasn't cut from magisterial cloth and neither am I.

Filov   Heavy lies the crown.

Boris   Crown of thorns,[11] more like. Is it really worth risking lives just to get a bit more room around the edges of a perfectly big country?

Filov   Your country, sir. Your people. Your responsibility. It rather does fall to you to make things right. Clean up your father's mess.

Boris (*petulant, whiney*)   But why?

Filov   Those are the mandates of monarchy.

Boris   But most of my people don't even travel more than ten miles from where they were born. You remember I visited that darling village Tsraklevtsi[12] last week – I chatted to that adorable *babitchka*[13] Stoyna.[14]

---

[10] This may seem silly, but it is these small details we have revelled in including; we found this anecdote in *Beyond Hitler's Grasp* by Michael Bar-Zohar.

[11] There is a biography of Boris III called *Crown of Thorns* by Stephane Groueff. This is the book the writers stumbled across on Sasha's Bulgarian grandfather's bookshelf which inspired them to write this play in the first place.

[12] Цръклевци – a village about an hour north west of Sofia in which Sasha's grandfather, whom she called O'papa, was born in October 1921. Exact date unknown because that was the way of things.

[13] Бабичка in Bulgarian means a granny/old lady figure who is not necessarily a blood relative.

[14] Though Boris III made a point of personally meeting peasants, he never met the real Stoyna. She was in fact Sasha's relative and was in fact shaped like a question mark and did not in fact ever leave the village. Not even once (or so the story goes).

Filov   I can't say I committed it to memory.

Boris   Oh I told you all about her. Tiny little thing, all hunched over, sort of shaped like a question mark.

Filov   Oh yes?

Boris   She told me she has never left her village.

Filov   You don't say.

Boris   I do say. Not once. Not even to Sofia. Are you telling me Stoyna really needs Thrace added to the menu of places she won't be visiting?

Filov   But think of the history books. Stoyna won't be remembered. You will be. I just want you to be remembered as a great king – a leader.

Boris   But not at the expense of the lives of my people.

Filov   Understood.

Boris   Now look here. (*Beat.*) There's an old proverb, Bulgarian: 'When the horses start kicking each other in the stable, it's the donkeys that get hurt.'[15] My wife reminds me daily what an ass I am, but an ass with a crown she says. (*Beat.*) I am the Head of State. (*Beat.*) I am the one in charge – yes? So nothing happens against my will. Is *that* understood?

Filov   As you say, your majesty.

Boris   Wonderful.

Filov   It's time to address your people, sir.

Vocal/instrumental sting: 'Mila Rodino'.

Boris   Do I have time for an emergency wee?[16]

Filov   The crowd is waiting for you, your majesty.

---

[15] Когато атовете се ритат магаретата теглят.

[16] Boris is reported to have described himself as so nervous addressing large crowds that he routinely took multiple toilet trips before a speech.

Vocal/instrumental sting: 'Ti si zemen raj'.

Boris   Have I made the right choice, Filov? Siding with Herr Hitler. I'm having doubts. That man is a tyrant, with a postage stamp for a moustache. Now Stalin, there's a facial curtain you could hide behind. My feelings say the Russians.

Filov   But your reasoning, sir. Remember your reasoning.

Boris   My reasoning?

Filov   Trust that brilliant logic of yours and your people will trust you. (*The crowd begins to chant, 'Boris, Boris, Boris!'*) Listen to their cheers. They want a great king – a leader.

Scene Three

Boris's Backstory

Boris *takes his position addressing his crowd, who break into applause.*

Bulgarians   Boris! Boris! Boris!

Boris   My fellow Bulgarians.

Actor 2   Boris Klemens Robert Maria –

Actor 4   Maria?

Actor 2   Yep – Pius Ludwig Stanislaus Xaver, King of Bulgaria, was not actually Bulgarian.

Actor 5   Not a single drop of Bulgarian blood ran through his veins.

Actor 3   But he *was* born in Sofia.

Actor 2   He inherited the throne after the abdication of his father Ferdinand the first.

Actor 5   Who was also not Bulgarian.

Actor 2   No. Ferdinand Maximilian Karl Leopold Maria –

Actor 4   Maria?!

Actor 2   – of Saxe-Coburg and Gotha was also not Bulgarian.

Actor 5   Bulgaria had been without a monarchy for 500 years –

Actor 3   They had been occupied by the Turks.

All *spit.*

Actor 5   – and the Bulgarian royal blood line was broken.

Actor 2   But once the Bulgarians had cast off their Ottoman yoke and regained their independence, they realised they wanted to be ruled by a king again, as in the golden days of yore.

Boris   Somebody's got to be on the stamp!

Actor 2   So a delegation was sent from European city to European city. The quest? To find a prince to sit on the throne.

The following section should happen at a quick pace; it's us fast-forwarding and giving the Cliff Notes version of history to bring you up to speed to the present moment.

Bulgarian Emissary   Hear ye, hear ye, the year is 1886, I am a Bulgarian emissary on a mission. We have a vacant throne in Sofia and if the crown fits, it's yours.

French Emissary (*pretending to smoke*)   Fresh out of princes in Paris I'm afraid.

Bulgarian Emissary   Ah well, never mind, perhaps in Austria?

Austrian Emissary (*in an Australian accent*)   All our princes are spoken for, mate. (*Everyone looks at him – the penny drops.*) Austria.

Bulgarian Emissary   All we need is one unspoken-for prince. Any prince. Any.

Boris *has been coaching* **Actor 3** *on 'how to be more Ferdinand'.*

Boris   Remember you're repressed. You *want* to hug me but you can't.

Ferdinand (*taking the acting note and turning to the* **Bulgarian Emissary**)   Couldn't help but overhear you there. Wondered if I might stake a claim?

Bulgarian Emissary   Got any royal blood?

Ferdinand   My pedigree is *rather good*. My grandfather was the last king of France, Louis Philippe d'Orleans, making Mummy a French princess. Papa was a German prince. Queen Victoria's my auntie and cousin Nicky is the Russian Czar.[17] Will that do? Ferdinand's the name.

Bulgarian Emissary   Are you white?

Ferdinand   Yes.

Bulgarian Emissary   Are you male?

Ferdinand   Yes. And I can ride a horse.

Bulgarian Emissary   What more do we need?

Actor 2   And so, Ferdinand became Ferdinand I of all Bulgaria.

Actor 5   Married Maria-Louisa of Bourbon-Parma.

Actor 4   And made four, in-no-way Bulgarian, children.

Boris   Of which I was the eldest.

Actor 4   Boris's father Ferdinand found himself on the losing side of World War I, and, ashamed of his failings, abdicated and fled the country.

Ferdinand   – to lead a media-free life.[18]

He leaves.

---

[17] Incidentally Czar Nicholas II was also Boris III's godfather.
[18] A nod to Prince Harry & Meghan Markle.

Boris (*to audience*)   I shall be psychologically unaffected I'm sure.

Actor 5   And the twenty-four-year-old Boris, abandoned by his father /

Actor 2   was crowned by /

Stefan   / I, Metropolitan Stefan, the Diocesan Bishop of Sofia and Head of the Bulgarian Orthodox Church, bestow upon you, Boris Klemens Robert (*is unsure and asks this as a question*) Maria? –

Boris   Yes Maria!

Stefan   – Pius Ludwig Stanislaus Xaver of Saxe-Coburg and Gotha, the crown and anoint you – Boris III Tsar of the Kingdom of Bulgaria.

Boris (*thinking it's his cue*)   I come –

Stefan   Your Majesty, as once I served your father, now I serve you.

Boris (*thinking it's definitely his cue*)   I come –

Stefan   You upon whose shoulders weighs the fate of nations and on whose conscience preys the lives of your people. (*Waits for* **Boris** *to speak, who has got his cue wrong enough times that he stays silent.*) Now it's your go –

Boris (*'oh me now is it?'*)   I come not to be served but to serve.

Stefan   God save the king!

All   God save the king!

Boris   God save me.

Actor 2   And so Bulgaria enjoyed a period of peace. For a time.

Boris   Oh what a treat.

Actor 5   But once again, war reared its ugly head.

Actor 4   Which is where we find ourselves now.

Actor 2   On a balcony in Sofia overlooking Battenburg Square.

Actor 5   With a not-Bulgarian Boris addressing his very Bulgarian subjects.

We return to the start of the scene, with an adoring crowd around **Boris***.*

Bulgarians   Boris! Boris! Boris!

Actor 2   And God how they love him.

Bulgarian Actor 4   Say it like it is, Boris!

Actor 2   Why do they love him?

Bulgarian Actor 3   Because he's approachable.

Bulgarian Actor 4   I just feel I could grab a pint with him.

Bulgarian Actor 5   Plus, he doesn't care about his hair – it's a mess, he's an everyman!

All (*each member of the* **Ensemble** *shout some variation of –*)   We love you, Boris.

This speech should be underscored.

Boris (*genuine, he may have been accidentally born to this fate, but turns out he might be great at it after all*)   My fellow Bulgarians. Long have you suffered under masters that have not been kind to you. Long have you been denied what is rightfully yours. And so the time has come to provide strong and stable leadership, to make decisions and new friends. Today I say to you, we have found that friend in Germany. With Germany's allyship, you will have your ancestral lands back. You will raise crops in Southern Dobrudja (*crowd cheer*), you will bask in the Macedonian sun (*crowd cheer*) and you will ride the plains of Thrace on your trusty Greek steeds (*crowd cheer*). Greater Bulgaria will be yours once more.

Filov *appears from the crowd to whisper in* **Boris***'s ear –*

Filov   Bravo, sir.

The crowd cheer and then disappear.

Actor 4   And that was Boris's plan.

Actor 2   'Ally' with the Germans to regain all the land his father had lost.

Actor 3   *Officially* ally with them.

Actor 4   But in word only.

Actor 5   And avoid actually fighting in the war effort.

Actor 3   He hoped he could ride out the war with no loss of Bulgarian life.

Actor 2   And he was *absolutely* convinced that it *might* just work.

Scene Four

Germany Ramps Up The Pressure On Bulgaria

Ensemble *sing – this is a very cheesy sorta old-school folky number.*

This land is your land, this land is my land,
From Macedonia to the Thracian grasslands,
From the Rila Mountains to the Black Sea waters,
This land was made for you and me.

Actor 4   Germany very quickly invaded Romania.

Actor 2   And Southern Dobrudja was returned to Bulgaria.

Actor 3   The people rejoiced, naming streets after Hitler and Mussolini.

Actor 5   But Germany was putting pressure on Bulgaria to fight in the war effort.

Enter **German Emissary**.

German Emissary   I am putting pressure on you to fight in the war effort.

Boris   Well, give me five minutes, I'll have a very good reason as to why we can't.

Ensemble *sing.*

This land was made for –
This land was made for you and me.

Actor 4   Germany felt Boris must do more to please The Führer.

German Emissary   You must do more to please The Führer!

Boris   But I've already appointed a pro-German Prime Minister.

Filov   Bogdan Filov.

Boris   And Filov has appointed a fascist Home Secretary.

Gabrovski   Petur Gabrovski.

Boris   What more could he possibly want?

Ensemble *sing.*

This land was made for –
This land was made for you and me.

Filov   Germany's invasion of Yugoslavia has been successful. They have agreed to return Thrace and Macedonia to Bulgaria.

Boris   Excellent.

Gabrovski   But not until after the war.

Filov   And on one condition.

Boris   Yes?

Filov   They are putting pressure on us to join the Tripartite Pact with Germany, Italy and Japan.

German Emissary   I'm putting pressure on you to join the Tripartite Pact with Germany, Italy and Japan.

Boris   But I've already allied with them!

Filov   Being an ally isn't always enough.

Boris (*to* **German Emissary**)   Are you saying you don't trust me?

German Emissary   I'm saying, our troops are marching to take land for you. Sign. The. Pact!

Boris   Fine! But not yet. I will sign it the second your troops cross our borders, not a moment sooner. Gabrovski, when should we expect them?

Gabrovski   One week today.

Boris   Dash it, Giovanna and I are in Italy, at a wedding. Family occasion, all pre-arranged. Back at the end of the month.

Filov   This will not please The Führer.

Boris   Oh I'll be sure to tell the bride. She's Mussolini's niece.[19]

All (*sing*)

> This land is your land, this land is my land,
> From Macedonia to the Thracian grasslands,
> From the Rila Mountains to the Black Sea waters,
> (*a capella*)
> This land was made for – This land was made for /

---

[19] Benito Mussolini had previously attended Boris and Giovanna's wedding on the 25 October 1930, which took place in Italy – and Mussolini registered the marriage himself.

Scene Five

The Law for the Defence of Our Nation

Filov   / Germany.

Boris   Sorry, what?

Filov   I had a meeting with The Führer, just to smooth things over. I suggested we start following their safety measures. Which excited him.

Boris   Excited how?

Gabrovski (*this is HUGE*)   He had double dessert.[20]

Filov   *So* excited he considers Bulgaria prime real estate for further rolling out his policies.

Filov *reveals the paperwork with a dramatic flourish.*

Filov   The Law for the Defence of Our Nation. You'll notice, I've made some minor adjustments to the German model seeing as Bulgarians are not Aryan.

Gabrovski   They're Bulg-Aryan.

Filov *is desperately trying to keep on track.*

Filov   Certain steps need to be taken to protect Bulgarian-blooded people in their own country.

Boris   Excellent. (*Beat.*) Protect them from what?

Filov   Isn't it obvious?

Boris   No . . . ?

Gabrovski   The Jews.[21]

Beat.

---

[20] This is true. Though he was famously teetotal, Hitler had quite the sweet tooth and there is documentation that when Bulgaria allied with Germany he had a second helping of strudel or some similar Deutsche delicacy.

[21] We as writers have tried to use anti-Semitic or othering language as sparingly as possible. The phrase 'The Jews' will be used by the characters of Filov, Gabrovski, Belev and Dannecker (and Boris in his hate-filled speech), but is never used in our world with The King's Players.

Boris   You can't be serious.

Filov   The feeling is –

Gabrovski   And I couldn't agree more.

Filov   – that we need to define the Jewish role in Bulgaria.

Boris   They're citizens like everyone else. My dentist is Jewish.

Filov   They're not strictly speaking Bulgarian, not by blood.

Boris   Neither am I.

Filov   But you're not Jewish.

Gabrovski   (*scoffs*)   Could you imagine?

Filov   They require special handling. They simply need to register themselves and their property. They cannot marry Bulgarian citizens or adopt Bulgarian children –

Gabrovski   They can't be in the army, they can't own cinemas, they can't train as accountants, and they *cannot* enjoy membership of The Pen Club.

Boris   Do we have a pen club?

Filov   I'm the President.[22] (*A breath of glacial air at how icily important this is; this is* **Filov***'s greatest love besides himself.*) Oh and one more thing – we'll take away their citizenship.

Boris   Absolutely not. They are my people.

Filov   You *did* ally with Germany.

Gabrovski   You did.

Filov   Romania, France, Hungary, they've all agreed. If we don't follow suit, we will be made to, eventually. The Führer has been quite firm.

---

22 Again, a little nugget we found in our research. Filov was also a renowned archaeologist, art historian and President of the Bulgarian Academy of Sciences.

Boris   I can be quite firm too. And I will be, just as soon as I've looked over thi– (*looking at the paperwork he's been handed*) my God the handwriting is awful. Gabrovski, is this your chicken scratch?

Filov   The penmanship is mine, sir.

Boris   Then I'm not sure what worries me more.

Boris *exits.* **Filov** *and* **Gabrovski** *talk privately.*

Gabrovski   I don't think he'll do it.

Filov   Perhaps it's time for a bit of the old iron hand in the velvet glove.

Gabrovski   But he doesn't wear gloves.

Filov   We carry on as planned. I've still got my man in Berlin. Just keep the rest of it hush hush from the king.

Gabrovski   What if he doesn't sign?

Filov   He'll sign. Let's make sure we're ready when he does.

Scene Six

Giovanna Gives Boris Advice

Radio #2 (**Actor 2**)   This is a Radio Broadcast from 'Europe at War', keeping you up to date. Today, news from abroad. In a vicious reprisal to the assassination of high-ranking SS official Reinhard Heydrich, Hitler's Schutzpolitzei have razed the Czech village of Lidice to the ground.[23] Meanwhile, 'Blitz Spirit' is alive and well in Great Britain as Fritz attacks from the skies. Bombing raids have

---

[23] An absolutely heartbreaking description of these events is included in *HHhH* by Laurent Binet, Chapter 240.

already destroyed much of London.[24] It seems nowhere is truly safe from the reach of The Führer. Anyway – back to Bulgaria.

A single coat rail crosses the stage, it's a tram chugging through the streets of Sofia.

The **Ensemble** *become inhabitants of the park and create a sense of peace and calm – evening is falling, perhaps a pigeon coo-coos,* **Actors 3** *&* **4** *may be present as two old men whiling away the day playing backgammon,* **Anka** *is busking with a cap on the ground at her feet.*

Actor 4 (*pushing the coat rail across the stage*)   All aboard – Battenburg Square, etc.

Giovanna *and* **Boris** *are trying to take a restful stroll through the park, arm in arm.*

Boris (*tossing a coin to* **Anka**)   Good luck in the arts.

Beat. **Boris** *walks away, staring at clouds.*

Boris   My love, I . . . I think . . . I think I might have made a mistake.

Giovanna (*faux-agog*)   You – a mistake? Surely not.

Boris   I myself was shocked, but here we are. (*Deep breath.*) It appears I have a Jewish problem on my hands.

Giovanna   You have a problem with the Jews? Darling, our dentist is Jewish.

Boris   No, *no*, I have a problem with the people who have the problem, *that* is my problem.

Giovanna   Careful, darling, you're going to give yourself angina.

---

[24] Feel free to update to a historical fact pertaining to the country or location the play is currently being performed. (E.g. 'American exceptionalism is alive and well as Rodgers and Hammerstein's *Oklahoma!* opens on Broadway, becoming an instantaneous stage classic, not like this rubbish – ahem – I mean, having joined the conflict in the wake of Pearl Harbor, 7 December 1941, a date that will live in infamy, Roosevelt announces that shoe rationing will go into effect in two days'.)

Boris   Giovanna, this law they want me to sign. It says I have to issue all Jewish people with yellow stars. Badges. They all have to wear them, all the time, prominently.

Giovanna   Has the law specified what sizes the stars must be?

Boris   No.

Giovanna   Then make them as small as possible.[25]

Boris   That's good.

Giovanna   I know.

Boris   That's *good*.

Giovanna   I'm not just a pretty face.

Boris   But then what's next? This law will strip them of their citizenship. What do I do?

Giovanna   The morning is wiser than the evening.[26] Sleep on it.

Boris   And in the morning they will ask me to sign it again.

Giovanna   A fly cannot enter a closed mouth.

Boris   So what – do nothing? Delay?

Giovanna   A drop carves a stone not with force but with perseverance.[27]

Boris   Giovanna. I'm delighted you're reading that proverb book I bought you for Christmas, but please say something forward-moving.

---

[25] The stars worn by the Jewish Bulgarians were the smallest in Europe, and there are accounts of Jewish people wearing small brooches with photos of King Boris & Queen Giovanna next to them. In *The Optimists* by Jacky Comforty, there are accounts of Christian Orthodox Bulgarians wearing stars in solidarity with their Jewish friends.

[26] Утрото е по-мъдро от вечерта. Meaning: Sleep on it. Bulgarians believe that it is wise to sleep on any important decisions, and the following morning you will have a better sense of the bigger picture.

[27] Капката дълбае камъка не със сила, а с постоянство. Meaning: Consistency may achieve more than physical force.

Giovanna   Ok. Go scorched earth on Hitler, stand up for what's right and be the man I know you are.

Boris   And option two?

Giovanna   Throw sand in the gears and see where that gets you.

Boris   I hate sand. It's coarse, rough –

Giovanna   – and gets everywhere, I know dear. Just spin them out in endless bureaucracy. It *would* be terribly Slavic of you.

Boris   It would, it would. But what would *you* do?

Giovanna (*beat – she almost answers honestly*)   What I would never do is make your decisions for you, my love. I've already been as strong and outspoken as the 1940s will allow.

Giovanna *exits faux-swooning.*

Boris (*to audience*)   Do you know, she's fluent in six languages that woman. Absolutely useless in all of them.

Giovanna (*from offstage*)   I heard that!

Boris *improvised interaction with an audience member, e.g. 'What would you do? Stare vacantly and shake your head at me, ok', etc.*

Gabrovski *and* **Filov** *enter.*

Scene Seven

Boris Avoids Signing the Law

Gabrovski   Time's up, sir. The Law for the Defence of Our Nation awaits. We need your signature.

Filov   To get the ball rolling on some of the security measures, we're establishing a Commissariat for Jewish Questions.

Boris   I don't have any questions.

Filov   You may not, sir, but the Bulgarian population certainly does.

Boris   Don't be absurd. Have you ever actually spoken to the Bulgarian population?

Filov   I have friends who are upper class, I have friends who are middle class, I have friends who are working cla– well, not working class.[28]

Boris   Well, I do. As a matter of fact, sometimes – on my days off – I don peasant garb, pop into villages and help out with odd jobs.[29]

Gabrovski   Seriously?

Boris   I thought it might allow me to better connect with my people.

Gabrovski   And nobody recognises you?

Boris   I just have one of those faces, I suppose.

Gabrovski   But you're all over the telly.

Boris   Yes but how many peasants do you know with tellies?

Filov   Sir, I'm afraid we didn't call this meeting to chin-wag about peasants. We simply want to process some – paperwork.

Boris   Fine. Leave it with me. I'll look it over in the car on the way to the ribbon-cutting for the new library in Plovdiv.

Filov   Sir! The Commissariat is poised to start work, we just need your signature. (*Nods to* **Gabrovski** *– the time has come to bring in the big guns.* **Gabrovski** *moves to bring* **Belev** *onstage.*) And on that note, there's someone we'd like you to meet.

---

[28] At time of writing this was a quote taken from UK Prime Minister Rishi Sunak. This can be updated to reflect a more recent out-of-touch politician from wherever this is being performed.
[29] There were historical accounts that allege he did actually do this, although we haven't seen any photographic evidence (yet).

Scene Eight

Belev & Dannecker In, Gabrovski Out

Belev *enters.*

Filov   Alexander Belev.

Gabrovski   Welcome back to Bulgaria.

Belev   There's been a cabinet reshuffle. I'll take it from here. (**Gabrovski** *doesn't leave.*) Go on, fuck off.

Gabrovski *exits.*

Belev   Your majesty.

Boris   I am well acquainted with your work, Bellend – Belev!

Belev   Well, I have just returned from The Reich –

Boris   *Gesundheit.*

Belev   – I've learned from the best and I'm ready to do what needs to be done. I'm going to be chairing a new initiative.

Filov   The Commissariat for Jewish Questions.

Boris   Yes of course and you're the best man for the job aren't you, Belev? Being Jewish and all.

Belev   NO. No. I'm NOT Jewish. My mother was Italian.[30]

Boris   That's so funny I could have sworn someone told me –

Belev   It's a vicious rumour. I'm not sure who started it, but I can assure you I'm ending it.

Boris   Can someone please clarify what is this Jewish question that needs answering?

---

[30] Belev was plagued by rumours of his Jewishness, much like Heydrich or even Hitler himself. Though we would never attribute causality, it is an interesting point of comparison.

Belev   What to do with them.

Boris   I'm going to need you to be more specific.

Dannecker *materialises out of thin air, scaring the crap out of everyone.*

Dannecker   What you need is a firm kick in the pants.

Filov   Herr Theodor Dannecker, I am *delighted* you're here.

Belev   Huge fan of your work in Paris.

Beat.

Dannecker   Hitler has personally selected me from the SS to inspire a bit of German efficiency in your operations. I am now the highest-ranking party official in all of Bulgaria.

Boris   Yes, and as you know Herr Dannecker – I am your keen ally. Enthusiastic as I am to host you, I really do think we have everything truly under control here. Your trip is not entirely wasted, however; the Black Sea is lovely this time of year.

Dannecker   I'm beginning to see why Adolf calls you a 'wily fox'.[31]

Boris   Because of my rakish moustache. And my vixen of a wife.

Dannecker   I suspect it has more to do with hoping we all underestimate you. I won't. You can trust me on that one.

Boris *and* **Dannecker** *are circling each other strategically. This becomes a deadly serious tango of sorts.* **Dannecker***, of course, is leading. A physical demonstration of their negotiations,* **Boris***'s avoidance and* **Dannecker***'s forcefulness. This is a big fun theatrical moment.*

> Of all the boys I've known and I've known some,
>
> Until I first met you I was lonesome,

---

[31] This is also the title of another text we used during our research – *Wily Fox* by Carl L. Steinhouse.

And when you came in sight, dear, my heart grew light,

And this old world seemed new to me.

You're really swell, I have to admit you,

Deserve expressions that really fit you,

And so I've racked my brain hoping to explain,

(**All**)   All the things that you do to me.

(**All**, *harmony*) *Bei mir bist du schön*, please let me explain,

'*Bei mir bist du schön*' means you're grand.

I could say '*bella, bella*' even '*sehr wunderbar*',

Each language only helps me tell you how grand you are.

I've tried to explain, '*bei mir bist du schön*',

So kiss me and say you understand.

The song ends with **Dannecker** *having the upper hand.*

Boris, **Filov** *and* **Dannecker** *listen to the* **Radio Broadcast**.

Radio #3 (Actor 5)   This is a Radio Broadcast from 'Europe at War', keeping you up to date. This just in – Germany has invaded the Soviet Union in a covert mission titled 'Operation Barbarossa'.[32] An ambitious change in tactics for the Axis Powers, and with the Russian forces depleted, who will come to the aid of the Balkans' poor cousin, Bulgaria?

Dannecker   Checkmate. There's no turning back. Nobody is Russian to help you. Sign the bill.

Boris (*patting his pockets*)   I'm afraid I don't appear to have a –

---

[32] This technically transpired in 1941, but we have condensed the timeline here and used this recognisable invasion of Russia. The purpose of this is to select an offensive against the Russians perpetrated by the Germans in order for Bulgaria to have made her bed, then being unable to turn to their former allies for aid.

Filov   Pen? (**Filov** *pulls a pen extravagantly from his breast pocket.*) Allow me to assist you.

This is a big theatrical beat. **Boris** *takes the pen and begrudgingly signs. Make this moment count.*

Dannecker   *Wundebar*, the Law for the Defence of Your Nation has been signed. Bulgaria is now in safe hands.

Filov, **Belev** *and* **Dannecker** *exit.* **Anka** *starts playing her instrument mournfully.*

Boris (*appealing to her and audience*)   What else could I do? My hands are tied.

He leaves the stage for the first time. **Anka** *keeps playing but then runs off when* **Belev** *and* **Lily** *start 'getting it on'.*

Scene Nine

We Meet Lily

Belev   Lily –

Belev *and* **Lily** *are having sex. They speak between forceful thrusts.* **Lily**'s *rubber-stamping motion being led by each of* **Belev**'s *thrusts. Each piece of paperwork has a copy. The copies go into one pile and the originals into another. NB for* **Lily**: *she is using the affair with* **Belev**[33] *to operate as a resistance spy.*

Lily   Yes.

Belev   Lily.

Lily   Yeah.

Belev   Oh God, I love how you stamp paperwork.

Lily   I told you business could be pleasure.

Belev (*thrusting between words*)   You – are – so – efficient.

Lily   I look after all of your needs don't I.

---

[33] Liliana testified to their affair in the Soviet People's Tribunal in 1945.

Belev   Oh yes.

Lily   Tell me what you want.

Belev   I want – I want – I want Dannecker to see what I'm fucking made of. And then I want a fucking promotion. And when I get it, I'm gonna show Filov where to shove his fucking fountain pen – oh – oh God – oh God – (**Filov** *enters.*) oh FUCK.

Belev *and* **Lily** *scramble to pull themselves together.*

Filov   I'll knock next time, shall I?

Lily   All done. The paperwork has been rubber-stamped.

Belev *indicates to* **Lily** *to hand the paperwork to* **Filov.**

Belev   Do I have your permission to start preparation on the round-ups?

Filov (*flicking through the files*)   Yes, let's start right away. As soon as they hear we've deported the Jews from Thrace and Macedonia, the rest will start to panic. We need to keep them calm – remember, it's harder to hunt a deer than herd a sheep.

Belev   Animal's an animal.

He exits, excited by his work as **Filov** *hands paperwork back to* **Lily.**

Filov   Send that down to the dispatch desk. We'll deploy agents to confiscate their valuables and commandeer their radios.

Lily   Their radios?

Filov   So they don't know what's coming.

Lily *goes to exit with the paperwork but turns back to* **Filov.**

Filov   Problem?

Beat.

Lily   No, Prime Minister.

Filov   Good. A new world is being born, restrictions will be imposed on anything that is alien to our nation.

He approaches **Lily** *and does something physical to try it on with her. She put out for* **Belev**, *why not him? It's not sincere. It's a terrifying power move.*

Filov   Bulgaria is joining the future. After five hundred years of being trampled under the hooves of larger beasts, we finally have the chance to make history, we will write the next chapter.

He exits, **Lily** *is left alone.*

Radio #4 (Actor 5)   This is a Radio Broadcast from 'Europe at War', keeping you up to date. The *Salvador*, a Bulgarian vessel carrying Jewish refugees fleeing to Turkey sank in the Sea of Marmara. Far from being the saviour to its 243 passengers and crew, the ship became their tomb. 204 souls, including 66 children, were lost.[34] In brighter news, the palace is thrilled to announce the birth of King Boris and Queen Giovanna's first-born;[35] a son and heir, Simeon II. Well done them.

Scene Ten

A Promenade in the Park

The same park as before, a single coat rail crosses the stage, slower this time. The pigeon coo-coos are more sombre, evening is falling. The two old men playing backgammon play slower now. The same busker is playing her flute – it is **Anka**.

Giovanna *is holding Simeon – a violin.*

---

[34] One of the survivors of this tragic shipwreck was interviewed by Jacky Comforty in his documentary *The Optimists*. We include it here because we felt it was crucial to show how the measures that the Bulgarian government had enacted so far were affecting the climate of the country. People were terrified and choosing to flee. As a result of this incident, Bulgaria's borders were formally sealed.

[35] For dramatic ease we have told an untruth here, Simeon was Boris & Giovanna's second-born – his older sister Princess Marie Louise was born in 1933. Simeon was actually born in 1937, but again to keep our internal timeline we have shifted this date.

Giovanna Darling, you haven't held Simeon all day.

Boris (*lost in thought looking at clouds*)   There's a cloud over there that looks just like Benito Mussolini – at an angle.

Giovanna Boris, you're not paying any attention to our son.

Boris Of course I am, he's there. Look just yesterday I gave every student in the country extra marks in their exams, all in honour of Simeon's birth.[36] So . . .

Giovanna Look at him. Hold him. He's this country's future.

Boris All I bloody do is think about this country's future. I'm having to fix my father's mistakes, eventually he'll have to fix mine. So I'd rather not make as many, if it's all the same to you.

Giovanna Boris.

Boris Whatever I do they back me into a corner; they jab me with another piece of legislation.

Beat. **Anka** *approaches them.*

Anka Your majesties – (*Awkwardly.*) Sorry to interrupt. I'm Anka Lazarov.

Giovanna Oh – the musician?

Anka The *Jewish* musician. My band is called The Optimists.[37]

---

[36] This really happened. Sasha's O'papa was failing school and, had it not been for the extra marks, would not have graduated. If he hadn't, perhaps he would never have left Tsraklevtsi, never emigrated to America and Sasha would never have been born and you wouldn't be reading this play. Isn't history fun?

[37] A reference to Jacky Comforty's documentary *The Optimists* named after a Bulgarian jazz band, some members of which were Jewish. Anka Lazarov was a real person and was in fact the aunt of historian Michael Bar-Zohar. Within this play her role is a composite of a number of resistance fighters.

Giovanna   Oh yes of course, I've heard you on the wireless! In fact, darling – we listened to their concert last night. I thought the costumes were excellent.

Anka   Thank you, your majesties. And, *mazel tov* for little Simeon.

Giovanna   Don't you think he has his father's moustache?

Beat.

Anka (*shooting her shot*)   I'm glad you enjoyed our concert on the radio, because Commissariat agents have confiscated mine. You are all happy to hear me play, but no one cares enough to stop what's happening.

Boris   I know you must be very worried.

Anka (*finds the confidence again to be direct*)   Worried? I'm terrified, we all are. We're being branded with these stars, but what's next?

Boris   Now see here –

Giovanna (*interrupting*)   If you and your family need to take a holiday, a permanent holiday, I happen to know just as many influential people as my husband. I could arrange the necessary documentation.

Anka   And go where? Curfew says I can't leave my house after dark, let alone my country. Besides, where am I supposed to go? This is my family's home. We've lived in the same house for a hundred years. My mother taught me to bake *banitsa* in that house. My father grew plums in the garden to make his own *rakia*. He defended our home in the war like his father before him. He was proud to fight as a Jew and as a Bulgarian.

Beat.

Boris (*to* **Giovanna**)   My love, would you leave us a while.

Giovanna   Oh thank God – do let me know if you should ever wish to hold your son.

She exits.

Boris (*exhales*)   Believe me I appreciate how difficult circumstances are, but to approach us in a public space and speak to my wife in that manner? If you do have complaints, I suggest you write a strongly worded letter to your MP.

Anka   I've tried that. I've tried everything and nobody is listening.

Boris   Ms Lazarov, I'm doing the best I can.

Anka   Are you?

Boris   I have a plan.

Anka   Have you stopped the restrictions on our freedoms? Have you stopped people looting our shops, breaking our windows, taking our names.

Boris   Wait –

Anka   There are people putting their lives on the line and you're whining about how hard it is to be king.

Boris   Who's taking your names?

Anka   What?

Boris   Taking your names, who told you? That's not public knowledge yet.

Anka   I – I can't –

Boris   No Jewish ovs, evs or itches. I signed it myself. But there's no way you could know that.

Anka   Just a lucky guess.

Boris   I doubt that very much. (*Beat.*) You are right. But you can only have heard that from somewhere high up. Who's your source? (*Exhales.*) If I'm to help you at all then I need to find out what is being decided in rooms when I'm not around, get ahead of Filov and Dannecker and whatever it is they're up to. If you know something that can help me, help me.

Anka   How do I know I can trust you?

Boris (*snaps at her desperately*)   What other choice do you have? (*Immediately regains his composure.*) Some would say you're more Bulgarian than I am, Anka Lazarov. But they happened to put me in charge. Help me.

Anka   She's a friend.

Boris   *I'm* a friend. I swear that on Simeon's life.

Beat. **Boris** *looks at* **Anka**.

Anka (*decides to trust him*)   I'm meeting her again tonight, if you want I can –

Boris   I'll come with you.

Anka   With respect, your majesty, you'll be recognised.

Boris   I'll wear a disguise, blend in.

Anka (*decides she has no choice*)   Fine, but it's just a party at a tobacco factory, mostly peasants, I'll lend you –

Boris   Believe it or not, I have just the thing.

Anka   *Gospodi*.[38] Please don't make me regret this.

Boris   I give you my word.

Anka   See you tonight then.

Boris   Wait – your informant. How will I know her, what's her name?

Anka *doesn't answer and exits.* **Boris** *exits.* **Belev** *enters and clicks to summon* **Lily**.

Belev   Lily! Down to business. Dannecker wants progress – I'm opening a relocation centre in Kyustendil.[39]

Lily (*shocked*)   What did you just say?

---

[38] *Господи* means 'Oh my God' in Bulgarian.
[39] The emphasis is on the first syllable: *Kyu*stendil.

Belev   Stupid little backwater town, we'll round the Jews up there and ship them abroad. Thousands of them. And I've found just the right place. A tobacco warehouse.

Lily   The one by the train station?

Belev   You know it?

Lily   I grew up there.

Scene Eleven

The Party

Actor 3   / A one, a two, a one, two, three, four!

Django Reinhardt's 'Minor Swing'. Everyone dances the horo. The party is built. **Actor 2**, **Actor 3** *and* **Actor 4** *are the party's band.*

Anka *and* **Boris** *enter,* **Boris** *wearing his 'peasant garb' disguise, hunched over like a question mark, a homage to Stoyna.*

Boris (*extremely pleased with himself*)   What do you think?

Anka   You'll blend right in.

Boris   Well, that's the idea. Where is she then – your informant?

Anka   Play it cool. Watch and listen. No one can know you're here.

Boris   Yes, right of course, of course. Because historically I wasn't here.

Ensemble *do a shot of rakia.* **Boris** *goes to shrink away –*

All   Opa![40] A one, two, three, four!

Musical interlude.

---

[40] *'Ona'* is an extremely versatile Bulgarian phrase that is primarily used in times of merriment, e.g. folk dancing. It can also be used as an expression of shock, excitement, surprise or to indicate a mistake has been made. It can sometimes indicate the feeling of 'come on'.

Boris   Opa! (*Coming back, whispering.*) What are we celebrating?

Anka (*loud to the room*)   The birth of the crown prince Simeon. (*Crowd shout 'OPA'!*) (*To* **Boris**.) Your son.

Boris   No I know who he is, I just think it's lovely. I must thank the host.

Anka   Boris! Wait! (*Whispers.*) The whole party is a cover. I needed to talk to her somewhere we wouldn't draw suspicion.

Boris   Right. Very clever.

Anka (*to* **Boris**)   Go, keep a low profile.

Musical interlude. **Boris** *awkward dances, etc. He is present but should not be distracting.* **Lily** *approaches* **Anka***, in a panic.*

Lily (*out of breath*)   Anka. Sorry, I was held up. I've just come from Belev. This warehouse has been requisitioned. Direct orders. It is to be emptied and repurposed for government use.

Anka   Are we arming ourselves against the Soviets?

Lily   Worse. Kyustendil is being turned into a deportation hub. The Commissariat, they need a holding pen, somewhere to round everyone up before deporting them abroad – who-knows-where. They're already sending Jewish families from Thrace and Macedonia to Belgrade. But if we act quickly, there may still be time.

Musical interlude. Music should speed up over the following lines –

Anka   This is happening faster than we thought.

Lily   I know, but it *is* happening. I typed up the order myself.

Music speeds up again.

Anka (*with profound worry*)   Someone graffitied 'we are coming' on the wall outside my house.

Lily (*reassuringly*)   Don't worry. We're still one step ahead.

Anka   For now.

Music speeds up again.

Lily *hands* **Anka** *the paperwork.*

Lily   This is the list of the first people to be arrested. Make sure they're not home when the call comes tomorrow.

She exits.

Boris (*joining* **Anka**)   Did she just say arrested? What's going on?

Anka (*angrily*)   Your government has drafted a list and deportations are about to begin.

Boris   They can't do that, they need my signature on every piece of legislation –

Anka   Stop foxtrotting with the fucking Führer! Your cabinet is in thrall to him, not you.

Boris   That's a little strong.

Anka   Oh sure, close your eyes, bury your head in the sand, pretend this isn't happening. Your life's not on the line after all.

Boris   I need to see it. Show me.

Anka   Come with me to the train station tomorrow morning. You can see it for yourself.

Scene Twelve

The Axis Of Evil Plans

Enter **Dannecker, Filov** *and* **Belev,** *they move into place and click their heels, they are reviewing a document – positively.*

Filov   This document confirms our delivery of 12,000 Jews from our supervised territories of Thrace and Macedonia to The Reich.[41]

Dannecker   Filov, Belev. It's not often that I'm moved to – pleasure? Your energy and enthusiasm have produced excellent results.

Filov/Belev   Thank you.

Belev   And, Herr Dannecker, if you'll permit me, I'd personally like to throw in 8,000 more from Bulgaria proper.

Dannecker   Well, I do love a round number.

Belev   I thought you might. That should be confirmation for Herr Hitler that we support the Final Solution.

Dannecker   It's certainly an excellent start. But, what about that king of yours?

Cut to – **Boris** *and* **Anka** *enter. The* **Ensemble** *enter with the two coat rails (these are the boxcars in Kyustendil).* **Boris** *and* **Anka** *in dismay and despair at the inhumanity.*

The guitar begins 'Shalom Aleichem'.[42]

Anka   Boris! This way.

Boris   What should I be seeing?

Anka   There!

The boxcars are moved into place as the **Ensemble** *sing.*

---

[41] This document would ultimately be the reason the Jewish citizens of Thrace and Macedonia were sent to their death, and was in fact the only physical document in the whole history of the Holocaust that was signed between Germany and any other nation. Dannecker signed in green ink, Belev in black. This feels inexplicably significant. A translation of the original by Bar-Zohar can be found on p. 69 of *Beyond Hitler's Grasp*.

[42] 'Shalom Aleichem' is a song traditionally sung on the eve of the Jewish Sabbath (Shabbat), it's deemed a 'greeting song', a greeting in of Shabbat, but also a song that includes the word 'Shalom'. Shalom is a particularly poignant word as it can encapsulate both the idea of 'peace' but also 'hello'. This is the first Jewish song we have heard in the play, which feels apt as we are about to face the extent of Jewish suffering that has and will continue to take place.

Shalom aleichem malachei hashareit, malachei elyon,
Mi melech, malchei hamelachim, hakadosh baruch hu.[43]

Anka   Now do you see?

Boris   I – I didn't know about this. I swear –

Anka   Well –

Boris *knows about it now. He can see it. They are lost for words.*
The boxcars are moved again to opposite sides of the stage, where
they stand skeletal and silent. **Boris** *too is silenced by what he sees.*

Hakadosh barach hu.

This line is repeated three times. **Boris** *exits after the second.*

The **Ensemble** *move back into the roles of* **Belev**, **Filov** *and*
Dannecker *as before.*

Dannecker   – what about that king of yours?

Filov   Fortunately otherwise engaged.

Belev   Don't worry about him. He's no threat to us.

Boris *enters; he does not see* **Dannecker**.

Boris   I wouldn't be so sure about that. (*To* **Filov**.) Cancel
the deportation.

Filov   Which deportation?

Boris   You would lie to your king?

Filov   I only sought to clarify. I would never lie to my
sovereign.

Boris   Kyustendil. An entire train depot has been emptied,
Filov – no goods, no trade. Why? Why are there boxcars
waiting? Where are they headed? Filov – what is their cargo?

Silence. **Boris** *is seething with rage.*

---

[43] Translation of the Hebrew: Peace upon you, ministering angels, messengers of the
Most High, sent by the King, King of Kings, the Holy One, Blessed be He.

Boris (*to* **Filov**)   Nothing and no one is to leave this country, do you hear me? (*To* **Belev**.) Cancel the deportation of the Bulgarian Jews.

Dannecker   Why?

Boris (*startled by* **Dannecker**)   Because –

Dannecker   Go on.

Boris   Because –

Dannecker   Everything is in motion. Hitler is watching.

Boris (*making it up on the fly*)   Because – I – I – I need them. I need them. For the – roads. I need them for the roads. Please do ask Herr Hitler where all of his troops are supposed to go when they get here? Oh sure, our mountain tracks are fine for a horse and cart, but try getting the *Wehrmacht* over the Vitosha mountains from Dolna Dikanya to Dolni Bogrov without some serious industrial revitalisation. Who's going to pay for that? Herr Dannecker, I only want what is best . . . (*He takes a deep breath and readies a salute.*) For The Reich.

Belev   No! No! No! Sorry, Herr Danneker, but everything is ready to go, let's round them up, ship them out!

Dannecker   *Halt's Maul!*[44] The wily fox is just toying with his food. Remember, it is a virtue to use every last fibre to fuel the Nazi industrial complex.

Belev   Yeh, well –

Boris (*putting him in his place*)   Industrial *complex*, Belev. Gosh, it could be it's just a little too complex for you. But Theodor and I do understand it I think, and each other? (**Dannecker** *nods.*) Good. Then don't worry, Belev, you will be given very clear instruction as to how to do your job.

Belev *seething at having been told off but keeping his cool.*

---

[44] German for 'shut your trap' or 'shut up'.

Dannecker   As you were.

He exits. **Boris** *returns to his throne thinking he has the upper hand.*

Filov   Belev, see that the 8,000 names on this list are distributed into companies and deployed into the regions to begin work immediately, we want to break ground before the weather changes.

Boris   You mean 20,000.

Filov   Sorry?

Boris   20,000 names will need to be reassigned –

Filov   I'm afraid you're mistaken. The 12,000 are from Thracian and Macedonian territories.

Boris (*growing in desperation as he realises he has been lied to*) No, that is Bulgaria. That land is ours. Filov, that's why we allied with Germany. To get our lands back. The lands my father lost. That's what you said.

Belev *laughs.*

Filov   Unfortunately those lands are not under your control until *after* the war. Look outside your window, sir, we're still at war.

Belev   It's all a little complex, isn't it.

Boris (*tantrum*)   But I am your king!

Filov   Yes, but not our Führer. The 11,343 Jews from Macedonia and Thrace are already en route for Treblinka. (*Beat.* **Belev** *exits.* **Filov** *drops his mask entirely.*) A word to the wise, some things are inevitable. Night follows day. Death follows life. Men follow power. So who will follow you?

He exits.

Scene Thirteen

Boris's Spiritual Reckoning

Ensemble *sings 'Avinu Malkeinu'[45] to honour the memory of the 11,343.*

Avinu malkeinu, Avinu malkeinu, Avinu malkeinu, chonenu va-anenu,
Ki ein banu ma-asim.

The **Ensemble** *move the boxcars once again. The wheels ring out against the floor like gunfire and death. This is the sound of thousands of people being sent to murder.*

Boris (*pleading to anyone who will listen*)   There was nothing I could do for those people – my hands are tied!

Aseh imanu tzedakah vachesed,
Aseh imanu tzedakah vachesed, vehoshiyeinu.

Actor 5 (*to the audience*)   Of the 11,343 Thracian and Macedonian men, women and children who were sent to Treblinka, only twelve survived. This fact remains a stain on Bulgaria to this day.

Boris   And on me.

Aseh imanu tzedakah vachesed,
Aseh imanu tzedakah vachesed,
Vehoshiyeinu.[46]

---

[45] 'Avinu Malkeinu' is a central prayer of the ten days of repentance which starts on Rosh Hashanah (the Jewish New Year) and concludes on Yom Kippur (the Day of Atonement). It is a prayer of supplication, an admission of guilt and an expressed desire to atone for sins committed.
This prayer is particularly powerful at this point in the play, knowing what is to become of so many Jewish people. In this prayer both the words and the melody evoke deep emotion as the congregation faces the year ahead – the Jewish belief being that in these days you are inscribed in the Book of Life or your name will be blotted out; it is decided in these days of repentance exactly what lies ahead.
[46] Translation: Our God, our King, have mercy on us, answer us, for our deeds are insufficient; deal with us charitably and lovingly, and redeem us.

Humming stops. **Boris** *is humbled. This moment of reckoning helps him to grow; he will remember what is truly at stake when he stands up to Hitler at the climax of the play.*

Scene Fourteen

Metropolitan Stefan

Stefan *enters; his music with him. It is a slow opening to 'Have A Little Talk With Jesus'.*

Boris *silently watches.*

> I once was lost in sin but Jesus took me in,
> And then a little light from heaven filled my soul,
> It bathed my heart in love and it wrote my name above,
> And just a little talk with Jesus made me whole.

Ensemble *enters and does a physical sequence cycling through three/four characters each, representing the hundreds of people being baptised.*

> Why don't you . . .

(The music picks up and slowly increases in pace.)

> Have a little talk with Jesus,
> Tell him about our troubles,
> He will hear our faintest cry,
> And he'll answer by and by,
> When you feel a little prayer wheel turning,
> You'll know a little fire is burning,
> A little talk with Jesus makes it right.

The chorus can be repeated two or three times to cover the baptismal section. Have fun with it. The audience needs a moment to recover from the previous scene and begin to feel there may be hope after all.

Boris   Stefan. My old friend. I have royally fucked up. I need forgiveness from the church.

Stefan   My child, can't you see I'm busy?

Boris   Too busy for your king?

Stefan   Some things are bigger than you, Boris. I've got hundreds of Jewish people to baptise before the Nazis get to them.

Boris   Come again?

Stefan   When Hitler's men are out there looking for yellow stars, what they'll find instead are newly baptised brothers and sisters in Christ.

Boris   It's too late for that, Stefan. I've already sent thousands of people to their death.

Stefan (*curtly*)   And here I am trying to make sure there aren't any more. Apologies and penitence are not good enough. Remember – you came not to be served, but to serve. And service requires action.

He turns away from **Boris** *and continues baptising,* **Boris** *considers his words. The music doubles in speed; it's jaunty and bluegrassy.*

Dannecker *enters with* **Filov** *behind.* **Boris** *remains silent, giving* **Stefan** *his moment to speak his mind.*

Dannecker   *Gott im Himmel.*[47] What is going on here? Why are hundreds of Jews tramping into this church?

Stefan   Everyone is welcome in the House of the Lord.

Convert (**Actor 5**) (*to* **Stefan**)   Amen.

Stefan   *Shkoyach.*[48]

---

[47] German for 'God in Heaven'.
[48] Definition by Aron Moss from chabad.org: 'Shkoyach is a condensed version of the Hebrew phrase Yeyasher Kochacha, literally, "May your strength be directed forward." Shkoyach is a versatile expression. It can be used to say bravo for a great sermon, good on you for being called to the Torah, or thank you for passing the herring. But the meaning is always the same. You have done something good, you should have the strength to do more.'

Dannecker   You expect me to believe that hundreds of Jews have miraculously repented their Christ-killing ways and sought conversion?

Stefan   The Lord works in mysterious ways.

Dannecker   If you think I will be taken in by your parochial theatrics, you are heartily mistaken.

Filov   This government does not recognise these sham conversions.

Boris (*authoritarian*)   I think I will decide what my government does and does not do, gentlemen.

*Ice chill. Everyone expects **Boris** to turn on **Dannecker**.*

Boris   But you are right. I have been stubborn and short-sighted. (*Turns to **Stefan**.*) A Christian is a Christian. And a Jew is a Jew. I am putting an end to these sham 'baptisms'.

Beat.

Boris (*to **Filov***)   This statement is to go out across the airwaves. To the whole country. (*Takes a deep breath, then stands and pronounces.*) The Jews have always had a profiteering spirit, which has inflicted heavy damage on countries worldwide for centuries. And so I say the sooner we rid ourselves of this pernicious Jewish influence the better off we will all be.[49] (*Beat.*) And in truth, my dear friend Stefan, I can't believe the patriotic Bulgarian Church would have a different position.

Filov   Well said, your majesty.

Stefan   You have been corrupted by this rhetoric of hate. (*To **Dannecker**.*) I will not rest until I find all those who need sanctuary. I will jump fences, I will break down doors, and if *any* train is to depart carrying Bulgarian citizens – we will *all*

---

[49] Boris corresponded regularly through letters to Metropolitan Stefan and other leaders of the Saint Synod in Bulgaria – this quote is an excerpt from one such letter. We decided, as this is a play, to lift the text and use it again later as a radio broadcast rather than confining it to the page.

of us lie down – Metropolitan and Rabbi, head to toe supine in front of that train![50]

Dannecker   Enough!

Stefan   With the measure you use, it will be used back to you.

Filov   Is that a threat?

Stefan   Matthew, Chapter 7, Verse 2.

Boris   The voice of the Church has been heard. I'm sorry you cannot find it within your faith to make space for the nation's best interest.

Filov (*proudly*)   His majesty has finally listened to his reasoning.

Dannecker   I will inform The Führer of your good sense immediately.

Dannecker *and* **Filov** *leave, sneering at* **Stefan**.

Stefan   I do not recognise the man you have become.

Boris   You wanted action. There's my action.

Stefan (*despairingly*)   God grant me strength.

Boris (*interrupting*)   Stefan, I can't cancel a second deportation, but I might be able to delay one.

Stefan   With those words?

Boris   They have to believe I've changed course. (*Exhales – imploring to* **Stefan**.) Listen. Filov and Dannecker report inside information about me to Berlin, yes? Well, I *know* that, so why not *use* that. Let them! Let them send back to German intelligence glowing reports of 'King Boris's new-found anti-Jewish stance'. My hands may be tied, but yours aren't. Shepherd your flock into the monasteries. Do what

---

[50] In *Beyond Hitler's Grasp* there are accounts of Metropolitans breaking down doors and jumping fences to stop people being rounded up and yes, of lying in front of a train to stop deportation!

you can in private, but in public – please, do not speak of me as a friend.

Stefan   My father's house has many rooms. And some of them even you don't know about. (*He extends a hand of friendship.*) I hope you know what you're doing.

He exits.

Radio #5 (Actor 5)   This is a Radio Broadcast from 'Europe at War', keeping you up to date. To the surprise of some, King Boris of Bulgaria appears to have capitulated to the Nazi party line. His latest shock statement now –

Boris   'The Jews have always had a profiteering spirit and so I say, the sooner we rid ourselves of this pernicious Jewish influence the better off we will all be.'

Scene Fifteen

Anka & Lily Ramp Up Plans

Lily *sits typing in the middle of the stage – using a flute as a typewriter.*

Filov *and* **Belev** *storm in.*

Belev   You don't seriously believe this, do you? He's afraid. He's up to something. I don't trust him.

Filov   Belev. I have never trusted anyone my entire life. I don't intend to start now. That being said, The Führer *will* require safe and speedy passage across the continent, and our infrastructure is simply not up to the task.

Belev   Horseshit.

Filov   As peeved as we both are about the Jews his majesty diverted from the deportation, they *are* building roads along the Greek border.

Belev   Fucking barely. They come and go as they please. Take breaks when they want, eat food when they want – they

sleep in their own fucking beds! What kind of labour camp
do you call that? We've not done enough. There's nearly
25,000 in Sofia alone, sitting there – (*Beat. Has an idea.*) Wait!

Belev/Anka   Lily!

The following section is played out in 'split screen'. **Lily** *turns over
her shoulder and these scenes play out side-by-side, with* **Lily**
*turning between her two different conversations. It has the furtive
energy of spies sitting adjacently in two cafe chairs like you see in the
movies, speaking to each other but under the guise of being solitary
patrons, hidden behind newspapers.*

Lily (*to* **Belev**)   Yes, sir?

Belev   Type up –

Anka   What's going on?

Lily   Anka – we need to come up with a plan and fast. The
deportation may be cancelled but the reprieve won't last
long.

Anka (*to* **Lily**)   Why? What are they thinking?

Belev (*lightbulb moment, sneers*)   Type up a detailed list –

Lily *turns to* **Anka**.

Lily   – of every Jewish household in Bulgaria for relocation
into ghettos in the provinces.

Belev (*to* **Filov**)   We only need the men to build the roads.
The rest can be deported.

Filov (*to* **Belev**)   Ingenious, particularly for you.

Anka   How many people can you get struck from the list?

Lily   I don't know, a hundred?

Anka   Lily, that's not even one precinct. And that's just in
Sofia.

Lily   They'll notice otherwise. It has to look like a clerical
mistake, not –

Anka   It's not good enough. When does this start?

Belev (*to* **Lily**)   As soon as possible.

Lily (*to* **Belev**)   But, sir – (*Looks at* **Anka** *then back to* **Filov**/**Belev**.) I'm worried. The public tide is turning against us.

Belev   Don't talk. You don't talk while we're talking.

Lily   I know. But you cannot relocate women, children, the elderly, to the perimeters of their own country. The people won't stand for it.

Filov   Clever girl. But don't fret, I have a tidy solution for our little problem. Do you recall the MP that was assassinated this morning?

Belev   What about him?

Filov/Lily   The assassin was Jewish.[51]

Belev   Oh good.

Anka   Oh God.

Filov   We can use this to our advantage. Call him a religious terrorist in the press, people love that. We can't restart full deportation plans immediately, but we can certainly begin moving them and arrest anyone who doesn't comply. Security is of the essence in the wake of this new (*very grave*) 'Jewish threat'.

Lily   But, Prime Minister, that is expressly against the King's wishes.

Belev   Lily!

Filov   The King cancelled the deportations out – but he didn't forbid moving them around.

Lily   But – we can't guarantee –

---

[51] On 13 February 1943, assassins shot and killed right-wing extremist General Christo Lukov – Prime Minister Filov decided to use this attack as a means of launching a propaganda campaign.

Filov (*he loses it here, he's almost frothing with excitement at his own future*)   The King's recent rhetoric demonstrates that he will have no issue with these crucial steps to protect the Bulgarian people. It will be the simplest of tasks to herd the last of the Jews to Poland's waiting arms, Hitler will hail me as a hero and I will . . . I will . . . I will treat myself to a nice new pen befitting my position in THE THIRD REICH.

Belev   Let's get started.

Beat – the atmosphere intensifies – **Boris** *speaks these lines live but it should feel as if it's on the* **Radio** *surrounding the Jewish people.*

Radio (**Boris**)   'The Jews have always had a profiteering spirit . . .'

Lily (*turning to* **Anka**, *terrified*)   They're mad, Anka.

Radio (**Boris**)   '. . . and so I say the sooner we rid ourselves of this pernicious Jewish influence, the better off we will all be . . .'

As this builds **Boris** *can play with rearranging these lines – as mad and angry and out of control as seems right.*

Radio (**Boris**)   'The Jews have ALWAYS had a profiteering spirit . . . and so I say the sooner we rid ourselves of this pernicious Jewish influence, the better off we will all be . . . THE JEWS HAVE ALWAYS –'

Filov *and* **Belev** *start echoing snatched phrases. This soundscape crescendos and becomes frightening.*

Boris *on the* **Radio** *builds and rises and becomes louder and more musical and drives* **Anka** *to action and to protest –*

Anka (*this is her call-to-arms speech*)   Enough talking! This is bullshit. The time has come for us to march, to fight! Knock on some doors. Don't stop knocking until everyone takes to the streets. If everyone with a Jewish friend came out and stood with us, those arrogant men in their fancy suits, safely tucked behind their desks, would see an entire country standing up to them. A country that does not agree with what they're telling us we want. Go, knock on doors, just pass it on, all you have to do is pass it on.

Scene Sixteen

Bulgarians Stand Together

Protest starts to swell.

Ensemble (*sing*)
　　Which side are you on, Boris?
　　Which side are you on?
　　Which side are you on, Boris?
　　Which side are you on?

Lily   My God. Look at how many people are here.

Anka   Bulgarians stand together.

Ensemble (*sing*)
　　Which side are you on, Boris?
　　Which side are you on?
　　Which side are you on, Boris?
　　Which side are you on?

Advisor 3 *emerges from the protest.*

Advisor 3   Your majesty, I have very distressing news.

Boris   Who are you?

Advisor 3   I'm Advisor Number 3.

Boris   Of course you are – how's the family?

Advisor 3   They're actually outside, sir, in the demonstration.

Ensemble (*sing*)
　　Which side are you on, Boris?
　　Which side are you on?

Advisor 3   Your people are not happy. What should we do?

Boris   I really don't know.

Advisor 3 *rejoins the crowd.*

Ensemble (*sing*)
  Which side are you on, Boris?
  Which side are you on?

Giovanna   Boris darling, what the fudge is going on?
Simeon's been woken up by this circus, people are protesting
in the streets, and now . . . Hitler's on the blower.

Boris   Oh what does he want now?

Giovanna   He's just lost to the Russians.

Boris *makes exasperated noise.*

Giovanna   And Mussolini has been deposed.

Boris   He'll be in a good mood then.

Giovanna   He wants to see you.

Boris   Ah. The sultan finally wants to see his talking camel.

Giovanna   What?

Boris   It's a proverb, from that book I gave you. There's a
sultan, a convict, a camel, takes about a year, it's a delay
tactic[52] –

Giovanna   There's no time for that, my love. He wants to
see you tomorrow.

Boris   Tomorrow?!

Giovanna   Tomorrow.

Boris   Friday the 13th?

Giovanna   If you say so, dear.

---

[52] A parable from when the Bulgarians were still under the Ottoman yoke and
everyone was equally at the mercy of a Sultan. A convict is to be put to death, and
convinces the Sultan to give him a year to teach a camel to speak. 'Impossible!' cries the
Sultan, but intrigued he allows it. The point being 'now I have a year, a lot can happen
in a year'.

Boris   Absolutely not! I will not fly on Friday the 13th![53]
No. (*Beat.*) Could you ask The Führer – is Saturday ok?

Giovanna   It's time to be firm, my little camel. Go scorched
earth on Hitler. Remember, you might be an ass, but you're
an ass with a crown.

She exits. **Boris** *is not reassured.*

Ensemble *start to sing 'Kaval Sviri' – perhaps it starts with
humming.*

Scene Seventeen

Boris Meets Hitler

*Hitler is brought on – a coat stand adorned with jacket and hat. The
light falls upon Hitler – his person is conjured out of shadow and
fabric.*

'Kaval Sviri' is sung interspersed throughout the dialogue. While
Boris *is speaking the song is maintained in an ominous drone.
There is no silence. Even if it's one hummed tone. Dread.*

Interjections are the voices in **Boris**'s *head, his memories, his
inspirations.*

   Kaval sviri, mamo, (titi)

Boris   Herr Hitler!

   Gore, dole, mamo, (titi)

Boris   This is not the occasion for one of your famous
monologues.

   *Kaval sviri, mamo, gore dole
   Gore dole, mamo, pod seloto*

---

[53] It is true that Boris didn't want to travel on Friday the 13th. He apparently said: 'On
Friday the Thirteenth, *je ne fonctionne pas!*' His junior secretary Stanislav Balan
managed to move the meeting to Saturday 14th on the pretext of an 'unforeseen
political emergency'.

Boris   I am tired of compromising. If you look out of my palace window you can see the Soviet flag on one side, and now your Nazi flag on the other. Little too much red for my liking.

Stefan   You came not to be served, but to serve.

Giovanna   Be firm, my little camel.

Anka   Stop foxtrotting with the fucking Führer!

Boris   Everything that has happened in Bulgaria is because of my words, my choices, my signature. I failed my people. I vowed there would be no loss of Bulgarian life in this war, and I broke that vow.

> *Kaval sviri, mamo, gore dole*
> *Gore dole, mamo, pod seloto*

Boris   Herr Hitler. I do not answer to you, I do not answer to my wife, I answer only to God and to my own conscience. It's time I said something important. Something that matters. We may have allied with Germany, but my people will no longer serve as collateral. There will be no more deportations of ANY of my subjects. Do you hear me?

> *Kaval sviri, mamo, (titi)*

Boris (*surprised but relieved*)   Thank you for your understanding, Herr Hitler. (*A glass is conjured from mid-air.*) Ah. You want to drink to mutual trust. Of course. Are you not having one?

> *Gore, dole, mamo,*

Boris *takes the glass and decides to drink. As the poisoned chalice touches his lips, the song erupts in a gallop.*

> *Kaval sviri, mamo, gore dole*
> *Gore dole, mamo, pod seloto*
> *Ja shte ida mamo da go vidja*
> *Da go vidya mamo, da go chuja*

Actor 2 (*to the audience*)   We do not know what was actually said behind closed doors; there was no official transcript of their exchange.[54] But as a result of this meeting, events were set in motion that resulted in the saving of nearly 50,000 Jewish Bulgarian lives. Also, Boris's death. But that was in the title. So.

Boris (*to* **Actor 2**, *almost pleadingly*)   At last my hands are free. I've untied them, just in time.

> *Kaval sviri, mamo,* (*titi*)
> *Gore, dole, mamo,* (*titi*)

Scene Eighteen

The Baddies' Comeuppance

Filov (*entering in a panic like a rat trying to scuttle off a sinking ship*)   Belev! Get all the paperwork together and have it destroyed.

Belev   I'm not your fucking secretary. Where's Dannecker?

Filov   He's gone. Hitler's had him reposted. Everyone is being called back.

Belev   Called back? Why?

Filov   Boris has cancelled it – Plan A, Plan B, all of it.

Belev   But Germany –

Filov   Mussolini's been deposed, the Soviets are closing in on Berlin. Germany is losing.

Belev   So, what's our next move?

Filov   Are you dim? We chose the wrong side, it's over.

Belev   No.

---

[54] There were however accounts from Hitler's guards outside the room that Hitler truly lost his shit.

Filov (*the panic is setting in, perhaps this is almost to himself in disbelief*)   I told you, Belev, destroy the paperwork. We must hope no one tries to invade. If the Allies turn up we'll be put on trial for war crimes and certainly executed.

Belev   But –

Filov   We gambled and we lost, Belev! Make whatever preparations you can.

Scene Nineteen

Boris Dies

Actor 2   Empowered by his moment of defiance against The Führer, Boris took a little retreat to his mountain hideout.

Actor 5   He had complained on the flight back to Sofia that he wasn't feeling his best, but he put it down to a rather stressful exchange with The Wolf.

Actor 3   His most trusted advisor joined him on his hike.[55]

Advisor 3   Your majesty, it was a gamble but your plan worked!

Boris   I suppose.

Advisor 3   Your people are safe.

Boris   Not all of them.

(*Beat.*)

Advisor 3   You stood up to Hitler. How many kings can say that?

Boris   Then why don't I feel better?

Advisor 3   You've just been under a great strain is all.

---

[55] The character of Advisor 3 is an amalgam of Boris's personal Dunovistic spiritual guru Lulchev, his personal aide Pavel Groueff (father of *Crown of Thorns* author Stephane Groueff) and a few other advisors and secretaries who often accompanied him on walks and retreats.

Boris   No, I feel quite unwell.

Advisor 3   Why don't you sit down for a second.

Boris *is in pain.*

Advisor 3   Your majesty! You need a doctor.

Boris   No, I need my wife.

He collapses and is carted back to Sofia and propped up in bed – holding his son.

Musical reprise – humming of 'Mila Rodino'.

Giovanna   How do you feel, my love?

Boris   Never better. It's just the pain in my left arm, the pressure on my chest and the difficulty breathing now. Here, take Simmy.

Giovanna   You do look a little green. (*She kisses him on the cheek.*) You should rest.

Boris   I really think I ought to –

He screams in pain.

A slow reprise of 'Mila Rodino' begins over the **Radio Broadcast**. *During the announcement –* **Boris** *dies.*

Scene Twenty

The Loose Ends Are Tied Up

Radio #6 (**Actor 3**)   This is a Radio Broadcast from 'Europe at War', keeping you up to date. On the heels of what seemed a decisive point scored against Hitler, King Boris III sadly passed away today, 28 August 1943. A nation mourns, joining its Queen Giovanna and young Prince Simeon in lamenting the loss of a great king, a leader.

Actor 3   The king's family had spoken of a 'typical Balkan death'.

Actor 5   Poison.

Actor 2   Of course they could not prove it. And Giovanna refused an autopsy.

Actor 3   The Germans started a rumour that the Italians were responsible.

Actor 2   Winston Churchill piped up and gave a speech warning that what happened to King Boris –

Actor 4 (*in a cod-Churchill voice for the Boomers*)   'will also happen to others who side with Germany!'

Actor 5   So for a while people blamed the British.

Actor 3   Usually a safe bet.

Actor 2 (*cutting back in*)   The official report said 'heart attack'.

Boris *sits up*.

Boris   No sorry I don't believe that, I'm the protagonist, I say I was poisoned by the Nazis!

Actor 2   Funny that; 'what happened' depends on who's telling it.

Actor 5   After Boris's death, his son Simeon succeeded him to the throne.

Actor 3   Soon after, Bulgaria was invaded by the Soviets.

Actor 2   Their historic allies.

Actor 5   The monarchy was abolished.

The **Ensemble** *conjure a series of montage scenelets that intersperse the narration.*

Actor 5   And the Russians established a People's Court.

Russian   The Official Soviet People's Tribunal is now convened.

Actor 4   Where they doled out vigilante justice indiscriminately to everyone who was involved in this complicated affair.

Russian   I am doling out vigilante justice indiscriminately to everyone who was involved in this complicated affair.

Actor 2   Dannecker was arrested, and took his own life in prison.

Actor 3   And Belev? A coward to the end – he fled.

Actor 4 *becomes* **Belev**, **Actor 5** *is the* **Factory Worker**.

Factory Worker   Belev? Alexander Belev. I know it's you. I was working on the floor of the tobacco factory when it was emptied. I saw you with the paperwork.

Belev   I think you've got me mistaken.

Factory Worker   I see exactly what you are.

Belev *turns to go and the* **Factory Worker** *shoots him in the back – the shot is signified through music.*

Actor 3   He was shot and his body was left in a ditch.

Actor 2   And so the Commissariat for Jewish Questions was closed, and with some well-placed suppression and brutal intimidation tactics, the Soviets felt content that the whole affair could be swept under the rug.

Actor 5   And very little was said of the Bulgarians' covert resistance against the Nazis.

Actor 4   Or the interventions of Metropolitan Stefan.

Actor 3   Or the people who protected their neighbours.

Actor 2   And Bulgaria slipped behind the Iron Curtain for the next fifty years and much that once was known was lost.

Actor 5 (*cutting in*)   That's the start of a whole *new* story though.

Actor 2 (*big moment*)   So, we end as we began, with us. With you. Because history doesn't stay safely tucked between the covers of a book. It is the stories we pass on.

Actor 4   The stories we tell ourselves.

Actor 3   Because we hear plenty about the good ol' days.

Actor 2   When *we* won the war.

Actor 5   We beat the baddies.

Actor 4   We fought them on the beaches.

Actor 3   We fought them in the trenches –

Boris   And we won. And we made *Dad's Army* and the last scene of *Blackadder* so nobody would forget we won.

Actor 4   But no story is ever quite as simple as that.

Boris   Least of all this one.

Clear signifier that this is not quite the end.

Ensemble *sings 'Avinu Malkeinu'.*

Scene Twenty-One

Anka & Lily Epilogue

We're back in Kyustendil. It's the golden light of afternoon. Perhaps we hear children playing. Everything has taken on a hue of victory and peace. Perhaps we finally have our fairy-tale Bulgaria back.

Lily   Anka

Anka   Lily. How will I ever thank you?

Lily   You never need to.

Anka   Will you be safe?[56]

---

[56] Lily was arrested and subjected to ferocious beatings at the hands of her Soviet interrogators. She testified in the tribunals and was acquitted but unfortunately died of her wounds a year later.

Lily   So many of you are leaving.

Anka   They say we'll be welcome in Jaffa.

Lily   You belong here.

Anka (*beat*)   Yeah – I can't stay here. I thought I could but I can't. In Jaffa, we won't have to think about the past, unless we want to, we can look to the future.

Lily   When do you leave?

Anka (*indicates at the waiting train*)   I will see you soon.

Lily   *Ako e rekel Gospod.*[57]

Anka   *Be'ezrat Hashem.*[58]

Lily *walks away and* **Anka** *goes to get her train but turns back.*

Anka   Hey! (**Lily** *turns.* **Anka** *sings.*)

   Mila rodino, Ti si zemen raj.

Lily *joins in.*

   Tvojta hubost, tvojta prelest,
   Ah, te njamat kraj.[59]

End of play.

---

[57] Ако е рекъл господ – 'God willing' in Bulgarian.
[58] בעזרת השם – The same in Hebrew.
[59] Michael Bar-Zohar recollects that when his family were making their final trip from Bulgaria to Jaffa, the train stopped at the Bulgarian border. He recalled that everyone got out and gazed back on the country that had been their home for so many years. Out of nowhere, a single voice started to sing 'Mila Rodino' until they all chimed in in a tearful farewell.

Supplementary Materials: Songs in the Original Language

Mila Rodino

Горда Стара планина,
до ней Дунава синей,
слънце Тракия огрява,
над Пирина пламеней.

(Родино) Мила Родино,
ти си земен рай,
твойта хубост, твойта прелест,
ах, те нямат край.

Shalom Aleichem

שָׁלוֹם עֲלֵיכֶם מַלְאֲכֵי הַשָּׁרֵת מַלְאֲכֵי עֶלְיוֹן
מִמֶּלֶךְ מַלְכֵי הַמְּלָכִים הַקָּדוֹשׁ בָּרוּךְ הוּא

Avenu Malkeinu

אָבִינוּ מַלְכֵּנוּ
חָנֵּנוּ וַעֲנֵנוּ
כִּי אֵין בָּנוּ מַעֲשִׂים
עֲשֵׂה עִמָּנוּ צְדָקָה וָחֶסֶד
וְהוֹשִׁיעֵנוּ

Kaval Sviri

Кавал свири, мамо,
горе доле, мамо, горе доле, мамо.
Кавал свири мамо,
горе доле, мамо, под селото.

Я ще ида, мамо, да го видя,
да го видя, мамо, да го чуя.

A kaval is playing, Mother,
up, down, Mother, up, down, Mother.

A kaval is playing, Mother,
up, down, Mother, near the village.

I will go, Mother, to see it,
to see it, Mother, to hear it.

A kaval is a traditional Bulgarian folk instrument. It is a
wooden flute that is end-blown and is primarily associated
with mountain shepherds.

Supplementary Materials: Some Things We Had to Miss Out

There is one name in particular that we tried so desperately to include: Dimitar Peshev, the deputy speaker of the Sobranie (National Assembly) and a former justice minister. His role, alongside a number of others, was integral to stopping the deportation from Kyustendil in March of 1943.

A key figure in the Jewish community in Kyustendil was Buko Lazarov (we instead meet his wife Anka Lazarov) who was informed by tobacco-warehouse owner Michael Abadjiev of the government's intentions to use his buildings as a holding pen, before deporting 20,000 Jewish people out of the country. When local Commissariat agents confirmed the plans, Lazarov leapt into action.

Lazarov organised a meeting with Assen Suitchmezov (a wealthy businessman), Ivan Momchilov (a local lawyer), Vladimir Kurtev (Macedonian leader) and many others, the most significant perhaps being Peter Mikhalev, an attorney and member of the Sobranie who worked alongside Peshev. Together they arranged a delegation of forty-four who agreed to travel to Sofia, although only the four named above actually made it.

The delegation went first to Dimitar Peshev – who attempted to meet with Prime Minister Filov. Denied an audience, Peshev and his compatriots instead petitioned Gabrovski, and as a result information was fed up the chain of command that plans had been leaked. Word must have reached Boris III because on 9 March 1943, Filov and Gabrovksi received an 'Order from the Highest Place' to stop deportations.

Peshev was arrested when the communist forces moved in, and imprisoned for one year. In 1973 Peshev was awarded the title of Righteous Among the Nations by Yad Vashem.

Other figures who played sizeable roles in the events during this period include Metropolitan Kyril, Rabbi Hananel,

Boris's sister Evdokia, Boris's spiritual advisor Lulchev and many others. It wouldn't feel right to tell this story without acknowledging these names, and more importantly the countless (and sadly often nameless) 'extraordinary ordinary' people in Bulgaria whose actions helped save nearly 50,000 lives in 1943.

We mention their names now because memory and story have power. We couldn't bring these people onto the stage, but we honour them here. Much like theatre making, the success of this rescue was the effort of many working in concert. Ernest Hemingway once said that every person dies two deaths. Once when they are buried, and once again when their name is spoken for the final time. Thank you for reading our play and thank you for keeping the story and the memories of these heroes from being forgotten.

We would encourage anyone who found the events in this play interesting to read the other sources included in the bibliography.

Supplementary Materials: Bibliography

Beyond Hitler's Grasp, Michael Bar-Zohar (Adams Media corporation, Massachusetts, 1998)

Wily Fox, Carl L. Steinhouse (AuthorHouse, Indiana, 2008)

Crown of Thorns, Stephane Groueff (Madison Books, Washington, 1998)

The Stolen Narrative of the Bulgarian Jews and the Holocaust, Jacky Comforty (Lexington Books, Maryland, 2021)

From Sofia to Jaffa: The Jews of Bulgaria and Israel, Guy H. Gaskell (Wayne State University Press, Michigan, 1994)

The Escape Artist, Jonathan Freedland (John Murray Publishers, London, 2023)

Border, Kapka Kassabova (Granta Publications, London, 2018)

Street Without a Name, Kapka Kassabova (Granta Publications, London, 2009)

The Optimists, dir. Jacky Comforty (2001)

HHhH, Laurent Binet (Vintage Random House, London, 2012)

A Unique Destiny: The memoir of the last tsar of Bulgaria, prime minister of a republic, Simon II of Bulgaria, Flammarion, Translated by Jane Coyner and Konstantin Saxe-Coburg (Stackpole Books, Maryland, 2021)

Printed in the USA
CPSIA information can be obtained
at www.ICGtesting.com
LVHW010721030624
782082LV00001B/146